KV-472-025

Making Observations:
The Potential of Observation
Methods for Gerontology

Edited by Andrew Clark

NUMBER 6 IN

**THE REPRESENTATION OF OLDER PEOPLE
IN AGEING RESEARCH SERIES**

THE CENTRE FOR POLICY ON AGEING AND
THE CENTRE FOR AGEING AND BIOGRAPHICAL
STUDIES AT THE OPEN UNIVERSITY

SERIES EDITORS
SHEILA PEACE AND JOANNA BORNAT

The Open
University

First published in 2007
by the Centre for Policy on Ageing
25-31 Ironmonger Row
London EC1V 3QP
Tel: +44 (0)20 7553 6500
Fax: +44 (0)20 7553 6501
Email: cpa@cpa.org.uk
Website: www.cpa.org.uk
Registered charity no 207163

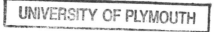
British Library Cataloguing in Publication Data
A catalogue record for this book is available from the British Library

ISBN 978-1-901097-01-6

The Representation of Older People in Ageing Research Series is based on seminars
organised by the Centre for Ageing and Biographical Studies, Faculty of Health and
Social Care, the Open University, and the Centre for Policy on Ageing. The papers in this
volume have been revised since the seminar took place.

Titles in the series:

Biographical Interviews: The Link Between Research and Practice, edited by Joanna
Bornat (No 1)

Involving Older People in Research: 'An Amateur Doing the Work of a Professional?',
edited by Sheila Peace (No 2)

Writing Old Age, edited by Julia Johnson (No 3)

Everyday Living in Later Life, edited by Bill Bytheway (No 4)

Recruitment and Sampling: Qualitative Research with Older People, edited by Caroline
Holland (No 5)

Language and Later Life: Issues, Methods and Representations, edited by Rebecca L.
Jones and John Percival (No 7)

Age-Old Prejudices: Research with Older People in a Discriminatory World,
edited by Richard Ward and Bill Bytheway (No 8)

Oral History and Ageing, edited by Joanna Bornat (No 9)

Printed in the United Kingdom by Henry Ling Limited,
at the Dorset Press, Dorchester DT1 1HD

CONTENTS

1

INTRODUCTION

The potential of observation methods for gerontology

ANDREW CLARK

OBSERVATION RESEARCH IN GERONTOLOGY[1]

The four chapters in this volume outline projects that used observation methods to understand better the social worlds of older people. They were first presented at a seminar in 2004 organised jointly by the Open University's Centre for Ageing and Biographical Studies and the Centre for Policy on Ageing, where the authors discussed how observational methods have been used in their research.

Collectively the chapters mirror the methodological, disciplinary and substantive diversity of observation methods in gerontology. This ranges from combined structured and ethnographic observations in a comparative study of residential care homes (Johnson); using video to research communication and interaction among older people with dementia (Cook and Hubbard); the theory and practice of observational research in the outdoor setting (Southwell); and ethnographic research in cemetery locations (Kellaher). The papers describe research conducted in a variety of field settings, from forests (Southwell) and cemeteries (Kellaher) to care homes (Cook and Hubbard; Johnson). In doing so, they are following an established tradition of observation in gerontology research.

Observation is now a staple of methods textbooks (e.g. Angrosino 2005; Adler and Adler 1994; Patton 2002; Robson 1993; Sànchez-Jankowski 2002; Wallace 2005). It has also been described as 'the fundamental base of all research methods' in the social and behavioural sciences (Adler and Adler 1994: 389; cited in Angrosino 2005 and Angrosino and Perez 2000). It is perhaps not surprising then, that there is a well-established tradition of observation research in gerontology. While this has predominantly been conducted in residential and care homes (e.g. Barnes 2006; Fairhurst 1990; Gubrium 1975; Keith 1977;

---

[1] Thanks to Caroline Holland for helpful comments on an earlier draft of this introduction.

Keith 1986; Shore *et al.* 1995; Stafford 2003), hospital wards (e.g. Jacelon 2004), or day centres (e.g. Salari *et al.* 2006), there is also a body of research that uses participant observation in neighbourhood and 'community' settings, usually within an ethnographic tradition (e.g. Fairclough 2001; Hochschild 1973).

Frequently, discussion of observation methods is presented as a brief precursor to a fuller discussion of participant observation, but this is just one way of conducting observation research. For observation methods can be positioned anywhere along the quantitative–qualitative methods spectrum. For example, in psychology and other disciplines with close ties to medical research, quantitative observations, designed to ensure standardised, controlled, data associated with the positivist 'scientific' tradition is well established. Qualitative observation in contrast tends to draw the observer into the lived worlds of those being observed. Thus conventionally, behaviourist and positivist research tends to work with standardised observation schedules and reach sample sizes appropriate for achieving statistical significance (e.g. Barnes 2006; Salari *et al.* 2006; Shore *et al.* 1995). Constructionists and post-positivists meanwhile have tended to favour the unstructured participant observation associated with ethnography (e.g. Fairclough 2001; Jerome 1992; Keith 1986).[2]

Beyond such epistemological diversity, observation also encompasses an eclectic array of 'methods', as indicated both in Gold's (1958) spectrum from complete participant to complete observer, and in Adler and Adler's (1994) typology of membership categories (see Figure 1.1).

---

[2] Ethnography is a diverse field of study that encompasses different assumptions about how knowledge about the world is constructed (epistemologies), the processes of constructing that knowledge (methodologies) and the tools to do so (methods). In referring to 'ethnographic observation' it is not my intention to infer that all ethnographic work follows 'post-positivist' epistemologies or adopts 'qualitative' methodologies but to emphasise those methods of observation associated with the ethnographic (methodological) tradition. In this I take my cue from Atkinson *et al.*, who state that, despite the differences and tensions of different ethnographic traditions, '[t]hey are grounded in a commitment to the first-hand experience and exploration of a particular social and cultural setting on the basis of (though not exclusively by) participant observation. Observation and participation... remain the characteristic features of the ethnographic approach. In many cases, of course, fieldwork entails the use of other research methods too. Participant observation alone would normally result in strange and unnatural behaviour were the observer not to talk... Hence, conversations and interviews are often indistinguishable from other forms of interaction and dialogue' (2001: 4–5).

Figure 1.1 Variations in observation research

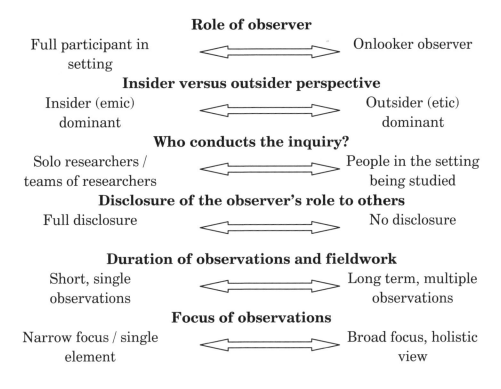

Role of observer

Full participant in setting ⬅———➡ Onlooker observer

Insider versus outsider perspective

Insider (emic) dominant ⬅———➡ Outsider (etic) dominant

Who conducts the inquiry?

Solo researchers / teams of researchers ⬅———➡ People in the setting being studied

Disclosure of the observer's role to others

Full disclosure ⬅———➡ No disclosure

Duration of observations and fieldwork

Short, single observations ⬅———➡ Long term, multiple observations

Focus of observations

Narrow focus / single element ⬅———➡ Broad focus, holistic view

Source: Patton 2002: 277.

Again this range is reflected in ageing research. A number of studies use unobtrusive non-participant observation using pre-defined observation schema, to assess quality of life or care within care settings (e.g. Coughlan and Ward 2005; Jacelon 2004; Macdonald *et al.* 1985; Shore *et al.* 1995; Wadensten 2005). Others use 'minimally obtrusive' observation to explore, for example, relationships between environment, behaviour, or social interactions (e.g. Barnes 2006; Clark *et al.* 2005; Salari *et al.* 2006; Salari and Rich 2001). Finally, some have used a mix of 'observer as participant' or 'participant observation' (e.g. Cooper *et al.* 2004; Fairhurst 1990; Hubbard *et al.* 2003; Keith 1986; Kontos 2004; Latimer 1997). In practice, observation research rarely follows such a clear binary distinction as shown in Figure 1.1 but rather falls somewhere between the two poles. Johnson, for example, draws on both numerical data collected in standardised, tabulated form and ethnographic narrative, while Kellaher's work, based on a conventional 'qualitative' mode of ethnography, resulted in some 1500 'contacts' between researchers and participants; a figure perhaps more associated with the scale of quantitative studies than detailed qualitative ethnography. Meanwhile, in presenting visual representations of their data, Southwell (behaviour maps) and Cook and Hubbard (video filming) highlight the difficulties of categorising observation data as either 'qualitative' or 'quantitative'.

SUMMARY OF CHAPTERS

The chapter by Cook and Hubbard discusses their use of video to understand communication of older people with dementia in a variety of care settings. Data was recorded on video to produce a permanent record of an interaction in context, but also to contribute to particular forms of dissemination. This included the filming of actors to re-present original data. Cook and Hubbard discuss the process of gathering, analysing and disseminating video data and outline how consent was negotiated during the process. They comment on how the video camera made the research meaningful and enjoyable for the participants in a way that pen and paper recording methods might not, and they reflect on the ease (or not) of eliciting participant interpretations from replayed video footage.

In the next chapter, Johnson revisits observational data from residential care homes conducted twenty-five years ago. Unlike much data 'revisiting' work this was not to reanalyse the data, but rather to re-examine the method. Working within the positivist tradition of the time, Johnson used three observation schedules that produced structured data. Johnson shows how these somewhat impersonal, 'objective' data were turned into 'meaningful' narratives through the process of 'writing ethnography'. But in presenting ethnographic data through oral presentation, Johnson considers the importance of performing ethnography, not through the 'explicit' performances of Cook and Hubbard's professional actors, but rather in the context of a research seminar. Johnson considers her own performance in such a setting; to 're-visit' data, recalling situations and experiences which through intonation and emotion can evoke in audiences something of the 'being there' in the research setting some twenty-five years later.

In chapter four, Southwell presents a way of using observation methods in environment-behaviour theory from the perspective of landscape architecture and design. While following in a tradition of observing individuals and groups in outdoor, public settings (e.g. Holland *et al.* 2007), Southwell demonstrates a use of observation methods from a slightly different perspective to those more accustomed to social science based gerontology. She considers the way-finding activities of older people outdoors to assess the appropriateness of environmental design, such as the location of signs or facilities. Through detailed consideration of older people's search for a toilet block, Southwell shows how different observation methods, including behaviour mapping, and 'selective' and 'diagnostic' observation can be used to identify a design-related problem. While the applicability of observation research is clear in Southwell's work, she also demonstrates how these methods can be used to explore the 'cause–effect' relations between environment and behaviour; a relationship that has been of interest to many gerontologists (Wahl and Wahl 2002).

In the final chapter, Kellaher looks at the use of observation methods in cemeteries. She considers how observation and interaction with participants enabled understanding of how the cemetery might express the continuation of social relationships between the living and the deceased. Kellaher weighs up the extent to which observation alone can generate description, analysis and contribute to policy formation. By considering data produced with and without additional data from (verbal) methods, Kellaher reflects on the degree to which observation can be considered 'credible' and 'valid' in its own right.

Although diverse, the chapters unite around common points of debate in observation research. It is to some of these issues: the benefits of conducting observations, the ethics of observation research and ways of representing observation data that I now turn.

THE BENEFITS AND PROBLEMS OF OBSERVATION RESEARCH

> We are continually impressed by the discrepancy between what is supposed to happen and what does happen, between law and fact, the institution and the individual, what people say they do and what they actually do, what leaders think people want and what people do want.
> (Madge and Harrison 1938: 32, cited in Sheridan 2002)

Madge and Harrison's summation of the benefits of observation methods still holds weight today. First, being able to observe directly the behaviour of individuals and groups infers a 'face validity' that ensures, to a degree, that social realities can be simultaneously observed, documented and analysed by the researcher. Second, observation methods enable researchers to document and understand the context within which activities and events occur (see Johnson). Third, firsthand experience of behaviours and events in their setting (or context) enables inductive inquiry rather than, necessarily, reliance on prior conceptualisations. Fourth, observation has the potential to reveal the mundane, routine activities that collectively make up the practices of everyday life that may escape the discursive attention of participants (see Southwell). Fifth, observation may permit the documenting of the life worlds of individuals who are unable to express their lived experiences verbally, such as older people with dementia (see Cook and Hubbard). Finally, it is often argued that through observation it is possible to understand what people may be unwilling or unable to discuss through other, predominantly verbal (interview and survey) methods, including sensitive issues such death, dying, and memorialisation (see Kellaher).

Of course, like any method, observation is not without problems. Some types of observation, such as that conducted within ethnography, have been criticised for their 'unscientific' methodology with concerns expressed about small sample sizes, difficulties replicating (naturalistic) studies, and the degree of subjectivity and interpretation required on the part of the researcher (Herbert 2000). While ethnographies of science have introduced ideas of how social practices structure the interrogation of data and theory in 'scientific' research (e.g. Epstein 1998), it is also important to recognise that some observation methods do strive to achieve a 'scientific objectivism', evident for example in clinical trials, evaluation of care treatments, and social psychology experimentation (see Denzin 1970; Robson 1993; and Webb *et al.* 1966 for overviews of unobtrusive observation methods; and Macdonald *et al.* 1985 for an example within gerontology research).

Still, the *validity of interpretations* remains an important element of observation methods. If our interpretations of what we see are mediated through our social and sensoral experiences, then there cannot be any 'objective observation'. To reiterate a well-cited example, it is difficult to tell if someone is 'waving' or 'drowning' through observation alone because interpretation requires shared meaning between the researcher and the observed. Thus validity in observation is not a given but rather depends on the interaction between the observer and the observed and the 'filtering process' used to determine what is seen and not seen and then recorded and not recorded (Sànchez-Jankowski 2002). What we 'see' as researchers is dependant on our own interests, biases and positions. Consequently, and as Kellaher notes, how we 'know what we see' requires interpretation and it is difficult through observation alone to distinguish between whether our interpretations are the result of what we believe we see, what we want to see, what we expect to see, or what we hope to see. Over the past two decades, though, the very notion of the validity of observations has been considered and called into question by the postmodernist critique of social research, which calls for more explicit reflection on the personal position of the observer (gender, sexuality, ethnicity, social class, etc.) as part of the interpretation process (Angrosino 2005; Clifford and Marcus 1986).

The second major issue concerns the belief that observational research lacks *generalisability and reliability* without statistical analysis to confirm the significance of patterns or trends beyond the workings of chance. Of course, the same criticism can be levied at any form of qualitative research, but when combined with concerns about validity this makes for a potent critique of observation methods. Certainly it is more likely that observations will be more 'accurate' for the group under study and generally remain unverified for extension to a larger population (Adler and Adler 1998). However, as the following chapters demonstrate, there are measures that researchers can adopt to enhance the validity and reliability of their observations. First, observations can be documented by different technologies, including video recordings (see Cook and Hubbard). Second, observations can be combined with other forms of data collection either to enhance their own validity, or to contribute to the triangulation of mixed methods (see Kellaher's chapter for a discussion of what can be learnt from observation with and without additional methods). Third, repeated observations can be adapted to 'test' emergent ideas and inductive 'hypotheses' (Keith 1986; and see Southwell's chapter for discussion of different forms of observation). Fourth, multiple observers can be deployed to assess the degree of, and potentially eliminate, observer 'bias' (see Holland *et al.* 2007 for an example of a recent observation study with multiple observers). Finally, different sorts of observations such as systematic, repeated, structured observations can be combined with descriptive accounts (see Johnson). However, as alluded to in Johnson's chapter, these criticisms loose something of their salience when observation is considered in a post-positivist research arena where different ways of reflecting on and representing data are considered. ✸

ETHICAL OBSERVATIONS

In the past, some have considered observation a relatively unobtrusive method because it relies on little time or effort from those observed. This is not to say, however, that the method is immune to ethical dilemmas. Two such issues concern researcher intervention and obtaining informed consent. If a benefit of observation research is to document the social world without 'interference' by researchers (for example by asking questions in 'unnatural' interview or survey settings), then problems will inevitably arise should the researcher intervene in this world. Yet in some cases, not intervening may be considered unethical and, potentially, irresponsible. At the same time, if observation research is to document social life 'as it happens', then data is arguably most 'valid' when participants are least aware they are being observed. This raises important questions about whether it is ethical for participants to not be made aware of their being part of a research project. This is more than a question of satisfying ethics committees, but rather concerns the legitimacy of covert observation techniques. While in ethnographic or fieldwork observation the distinction between overt and covert research is often a matter a degree of divulgence on the part of the researcher (for example when confronted as to his or her purpose for being in the setting), some research has relied almost exclusively on researchers concealing their role. Proponents argue that observing without informing participants has produced useful insights into marginal, hidden activities (of which perhaps Humphreys' [1975] study is the most widely known), or work on 'deviant' groups such as right-wing political groups (Fielding 1982; Lauder 2003) or religious groups (Alfred 1976). Critics however question the moral integrity of such work (Herrera 1999), with some considering it a 'gross invasion of personal privacy' (Homan and Bulmer 1982: 109–110).

Yet obtaining informed consent is not always possible or desirable. For example, in some settings (such as among crowds or in public spaces) it may be impossible to obtain consent from all those present, and there are also persuasive arguments about the legitimacy of observing individuals in public spaces. Yet as many have commented, public space is often appropriated by social groups as their own 'private space' (Holland *et al.* 2007). And of course, there is a difference between not informing participants (Southwell), and deceiving them, even if some do not always explicitly recognise such a distinction (Lauder 2003).

In practice, informed consent is not a fixed, one-off agreement, but rather one that can change over time. Ideas of what constitutes ethical informed consent can also change. As Johnson notes here, 'present day researchers may well express amazement that in 1981 [she] was granted access to bedrooms and bathrooms as well as communal living and dining areas'. But should lack of informed consent at the time of data collection prevent researchers from returning to old data (either their own or others)? Second, as Cook and Hubbard demonstrate, it may not always be possible to obtain written consent, particularly when participants may have difficulty comprehending what it is they are being informed of and consenting to. And finally, as Cook and Hubbard also comment, consent is perhaps more ethically 'appropriate' if it is re-negotiated over the course of the research process.

(RE)PRESENTING OBSERVATION DATA

For much of their history, observational methods have developed in a framework designed to achieve a kind of objective rigour or absolute truth, usually through the production of quantifiable data. The postmodernist critique of the 'objective' observer and subsequent 'data as truth' has prompted considerable debate about the role of (mainly ethnographic-orientated) observation in achieving an authoritative, scientific truth (Clifford and Marcus 1986). Consequently, it has become increasingly common for observers to consider their own position in the research field. In part this is so as to develop greater insight into the production of observation data, not in order to produce more 'truthful' accounts of what we observe, but rather to understand how those accounts are created (Angrosino and Pérez 2000). Outside of positivist schools of thought, there are perhaps now few researchers who might claim to be able to 'capture the truth' of a setting or interaction either at all or through observation alone. As critique of (ethnographic based) observation has inspired observers to question the processes behind the production of their observations, a trend has emerged that re-posits the role of the observer as evoker rather than interpreter of ethnographic accounts of social groups and settings (Clifford and Marcus 1986). This has encouraged some to consider alternative ways of conceptualising the practices and politics of the research process, including ways in which data and findings are presented or 'performed'. Thus while not adopting an explicitly performative ethnography, Johnson distinguishes between 'doing', 'composing' and 'performing' ethnography and reflects on her own ethnographic 'performance' in a seminar setting, and Cook and Hubbard discuss the dramatising of research findings for dissemination.

The application of new technologies to record potential 'data', as Cook and Hubbard's chapter implies, presents opportunities to record 'reality in ways that could be said to transcend the individual researcher's limited capacity to interpret' (Angrosino and Pérez 2000: 696). Such technologies make it possible for any number of researchers to observe repeatedly the minutiae of interactions over and over again: repeatedly re-observing, re-analysing, even re-theorising the same scene. The use of video recordings enables researchers to document and analyse different verbal and non-verbal behaviours that might be missed by the human observer, during participant observation. An additional benefit is the way that video can engage participants in the research process, potentially opening up academic research to a wider audience. But as Cook and Hubbard warn, it is important not to approach data recorded through such means as any more or less 'truthful' than other forms of data, but rather remain aware of their existence as 'social and technological constructions'.

SOME REFLECTIONS ON THE PROSPECTS FOR OBSERVATION METHODS IN GERONTOLOGY RESEARCH

Making observations in social and cultural gerontology

Despite placing so much emphasis on the importance of observation in understanding the social world, it is perhaps curious that gerontologists do not make more explicit use of observation methods. For while participant observation is central to ethnography, attention appears to be more focused on 'participation', for example of researcher-interactions with the participant community through interview and survey methods than on 'observation' per se. Indeed, observation appears to languish behind interview and survey methods as the primary focuses of data collection in social and cultural gerontology. For instance, at a recent international symposium on cultural gerontology,[3] only six of the sixty-four abstracts of presented papers made reference to 'observation', 'participant observation' or even 'ethnography', and of these just two explicitly mentioned the use of 'observation' methods. This is not to say

---

[3] *Current and Future Pasts: The 5ᵗʰ International Symposium on Cultural Gerontology,* Milton Keynes, 19–21 May 2005. Papers drawing on data collected from the Mass-observation archive are excluded from this figure.

that other papers did not report on research that also produced observation data (visual impairment not withstanding, it is difficult for researchers to conduct face-to-face surveys, interviews and focus groups without also taking note of visual stimuli such as setting, body language, appearance of participants, etc.), but rather that observation is seldom made explicit in discussions of the methods of data collection.

The following chapters demonstrate the potential for observation methods in gerontology. Observation provides the opportunity for gerontologists to document the social lives of older people as they are 'being made' and unlike other methods, does not rely on the quality of participants' memories or risk participants succumbing to self-reported bias when faced with difficult or sensitive questions. Regardless of the form observation may take, it has the potential to reveal some of the ways in which the structured aspects of social life are played out in the social practices and particularities of the everyday lives of older people. If this is what critical and social branches of gerontology are about (Chappell and Penning 2001; Phillipson 2003) then observation as part of ethnographic and fieldwork endeavours should play as important a role as interviews and surveys.

Making wider observations

On the capabilities of observation methods to contribute to theory-building or generalisation beyond the sampled populations, Angrosino (2005: 741) is inclined to support Abu-Lughod's (1991: 154) call for observation research to commit to 'the ethnography of the particular'. In doing so, rather than approach the observation of a social group as some kind of 'microcosm' of wider society, researchers who favour qualitative observation will increasingly use the method to develop more nuanced accounts of particular people in particular places, with 'the focus being on individuals and their ever-changing relationships rather than on supposedly homogenous, coherent, patterned, and ... timeless nature of the supposed group' (Angrosino 2005: 741). As discussed above, observation research tends to fall into one of two positions: either quantitative techniques using structured observation schedules, or qualitative techniques adopting a more narrative structure. Yet this, considered alongside calls for observation to contribute to an 'ethnography of the particular' (rather than 'generalisable theory-building') suggests that observation methods sit somewhat uneasily between a positivistic school of inquiry that tend to favour quantitative methods, and those more inclined to reject a search for a single 'truth' while adopting qualitative ways of inquiring about the social world. Yet while Angrosino (2005: 741) predicts that observational techniques will 'find a home in a redefined genre of genre of cultural studies', as Figure 1.1 indicates there is opportunity for multiple perspectives to make use of observation methods; surely a useful attribute given the inter and multi disciplinary status of gerontology (Alkema and Alley 2006; Ferraro 2006; Kendig 2003). However, if different branches of gerontology are to develop observation methods, it is likely to become increasingly important that researchers situate these observations in their epistemological as well as 'real world' contexts.

Making observations in different settings

For good reason, the environmental context for much research in gerontology are residential and (perhaps to a declining extent) institutional settings or 'retirement communities' (Kendig 2003). These settings also tend to provide the research context for observation methods. Of course as a demographic group older people do not restrict themselves to such places. Yet gerontology appears somewhat reluctant to explore the lives of older people in other places, or at least to do so using observation methods. This is somewhat ironic given the amount of research conducted in public spaces using different observation methods. Low (2000) for instance combined participant observation and observational behaviour maps with ethnographic interviews and archived data to present a detailed ethnography of the importance of public squares and plazas to urban life in Costa Rica. And in the UK, Holland and colleagues (2007) have completed a twelve-month longitudinal study of intergenerational social interactions in public spaces across one British town using a combination of structured and semi-structured observation techniques completed by a team of lay researchers. Given that older people appear conspicuous by their absence from the literature on public space, other than cursory mentions *vis-a-vis* the activities and representations of younger people, there appears to be scope for more research exploring the position, attitudes and activities, of older people in socially heterogeneous settings such as shopping centres, mixed residential neighbourhoods, gyms, libraries, parks and other public spaces. Kellaher's and Southwell's chapters in this volume contribute to the diversity of environmental settings for observation research in gerontology and in doing so support Holland *et al.*'s (2007) point that observation techniques are well suited to providing insight into the lives of older people regardless of settings. Consequently, observation methods appear well placed to support the response to the 'astonishing paucity' of gerontology research on environments such as neighbourhoods, regions and rural areas (Kendig 2003: 612), or contribute to Phillipson's call for 'an urban ethnography that can capture the essence of ageing within cities' (2004: 970).

CONCLUSION

Revisiting archived observation data (see Johnson) and the development and implementation of new technologies to assist in the collection of observation data (see Cook and Hubbard) are beginning to impact on the debates discussed here. Concerns about research ethics, obtaining consent, preserving participant anonymity, and the potential to repeatedly re-interpret the same observation scene, along with the ability for researchers to more easily re-visit old data and reassess the context of its collection will inevitably affect how we conduct observation research. Observation research is a broad field and while the following chapters demonstrate the variety of disciplinary contexts, field-settings, applications and methods of making observations, they also hint at some of the ways in which underlying epistemological and methodological debates may emerge through research with older people.

REFERENCES

Abu-Lughod, L. (1991) Writing against culture, in Fox, R. (ed.) *Recapturing Anthropology: Working in the Present,* Santa Fe, NM: School of American Research Press, pp. 137–162.

Adler, P. and Adler, P. (1994) Observational techniques, in Denzin, N. and Lincoln, Y. (eds) *The Sage Handbook of Qualitative Research,* 1st edition, Thousand Oaks, CA: Sage, pp. 377–392.

Adler, P. and Adler, P. (1998) Observational techniques, in Denzin, N. and Lincoln, Y. (eds) *Collecting and Interpreting Qualitative Data,* Thousand Oaks, CA: Sage, pp. 79–109.

Alfred, R. (1976) The church of Satan, in Glock, C. and Bellah, R. (eds) *The New Religious Consciousness,* Berkeley, CA: University of California Press, pp. 180–202.

Alkema, G. and Alley, D. (2006) Gerontology's future: an integrative model for disciplinary advancement, *The Gerontologist* 46(5): 574–582.

Angrosino, M. (2005) Recontextualizing observation: ethnography, pedagogy, and the prospects for a progressive political agenda, in Denzin, N. and Lincoln, Y. (eds) *The Sage Handbook of Qualitative Research,* 3rd edition, Thousand Oaks, CA: Sage, pp. 729–745.

Angrosino, M. and Pérez, K. (2000) Rethinking observation: from method to context, in Denzin, N. and Lincoln, Y. (eds) *The Sage Handbook of Qualitative Research,* 2nd edition, Thousand Oaks, CA: Sage, pp. 673–702.

Atkinson, P., Coffey, A., Delamont, S., Lofland, J. and Lofland, L. (2001) Editorial introduction, in Atkinson, P., Coffey, A., Delamont, S., Lofland, J. and Lofland, L. (eds) *Handbook of Ethnography,* London: Sage, pp. 1–7.

Barnes, S. (2006) Space, choice and control, and quality of life in care settings for older people, *Environment and Behaviour* 38(5): 589–604.

Chappell, N. and Penning, M. (2001) Sociology of aging in Canada: issues for the millennium, *Canadian Journal of Aging* 20: 82–110.

Clark, A., Holland, C., Peace, S., and Katz, J. (2005) Social interactions in urban public places: participative method and recruitment strategies, in Holland, C. (ed.) *Recruitment and Sampling: Qualitative Research with Older People,* London: Centre for Policy on Ageing/The Open University, pp. 72–83.

Clifford, J. and Marcus, G. (eds) (1986) *Writing Culture,* Berkeley, CA: University of California Press.

Cooper, J., Lewis, R. and Urquhart, C. (2004) Using participant or non-participant observation to explain information behaviour, *Information Research* 9(4), paper 184.

Coughlan, R. and Ward, L. (2005) Experiences of recently relocated residents of a long-term care facility in Ontario: assessing quality qualitatively, *International Journal of Nursing Studies* 44(1): 47–57.

Denzin, N. (1970) Unobtrusive measures: the quest for triangulated and non-reactive methods of observations, in Denzin, N. (ed.) *The Research Act: A Theoretical Introduction to Sociological Methods,* Chicago, IL: Aldine Publishing, pp. 256–288.

Epstein, S. (1998) *Impure Science: AIDS, Activism and the Politics of Knowledge,* Berkeley, CA: University of California Press.

Fairclough, C. (2001) 'Those people' and troubles talk: social typing and community construction in senior public housing, *Journal of Aging Studies* 15: 333–350.

14

Fairhurst, E. (1990) Doing ethnography in a geriatric unit, in Peace, S. (ed.) *Researching Social Gerontology: Concepts, Methods and Issues,* London: Sage, pp. 101–114.

Ferraro, K. (2006) Imagining the disciplinary advancement of gerontology: whither the tipping point?, *The Gerontologist* 46(5): 571–573.

Fielding, N. (1982) Observational research on the National Front, in Bulmer, M. (ed.) *Social Research Ethics: An Examination of the Merits of Covert Participant Observation,* New York: Holmes and Meier, pp. 80–104.

Gold, R. (1958) Roles in sociological field observation, *Social Forces* 36: 217–223.

Gubrium, J. (1975) *Living and Dying in Murray Manor,* New York: St Martins Press.

Herbert, S. (2000) For ethnography, *Progress in Human Geography* 24(4): 550–568.

Herrera, C. (1999) Two arguments for 'covert methods' in social research, *British Journal of Sociology* 50(2): 331–344.

Hochschild, A. (1973) *The Unexpected Community: Portrait of an Old Age Subculture,* Berkeley, CA: University of California Press.

Holland, C., Clark, A., Katz, J. and Peace, S. (2007) *Social Interactions in Urban Public Places,* Bristol: Policy Press/Joseph Rowntree Foundation.

Homan, R. and Bulmer, M. (1982) On the merits of covert methods: a dialogue, in Bulmer, M. (ed.) *Social Research Ethics: An Examination of the Merits of Covert Participant Observation,* New York: Holmes and Meier, pp. 105–121.

Hubbard, G., Tester, S. and Downs, M. (2003) Meaningful social interactions between older people in institutional care settings, *Ageing & Society* 23: 99–114.

Humphreys, L. (1975) *Tearoom Trade: Impersonal Sex in Public Places,* New York: Aldine.

Jacelon, C. S. (2004) Managing personal integrity: the process of hospitalization for elders, *Journal of Advanced Nursing* 46(5): 549–557.

Jerome, D. (1992) *Good Company: An Anthropological Study of Old People in Groups,* Edinburgh: Edinburgh University Press.

Keith, J. (1977) *Old People, New Lives: Community Creation in a Retirement Residence,* Chicago, IL: University of Chicago Press.

Keith, J. (1986) Participant observation, in Fry, C. and Keith, J. (eds) *New Methods for Old Age Research,* South Hadley, MA: Bergin and Garvey, pp. 1–20.

Kendig, H. (2003) Directions in environmental gerontology: a multidisciplinary field, *The Gerontologist* 43(5): 611–615.

Kontos, P. (2004) Ethnographic reflections on selfhood, embodiment and Alzheimer's disease, *Ageing & Society* 24: 829–849.

Latimer, J. (1997) Figuring identities: older people, medicine and time, in Jamieson, A., Harper, S. and Victor, C. (eds) *Critical Approaches to Ageing and Later Life,* Buckingham: Open University Press, pp. 143–159.

Lauder, M. (2003) Covert participant observation of a deviant community: justifying the use of deception, *Journal of Contemporary Religions* 18(2): 185–196.

Loftland, J. (1971) *Analyzing Social Settings,* Belmont, CA: Wadsworth.

Low, S. (2000) *On the Plaza: The Politics of Public Space and Culture* Austin, TX: University of Texas Press.

Macdonald, A., Craig, T. and Warner, L. (1985) The development of a short observation method for the study of activity and contacts of old people in residential settings, *Psychological Medicine* 15: 167–172.

Madge, C. and Harrisson, T. (1938) *First Year's Work by Mass-Observation,* London: Lindsay Drummond.

Patton, M. (2002) *Qualitative Research and Evaluation Methods,* 3rd edition, Thousand Oaks, CA: Sage.

Phillipson, C. (2003) Globalisation and the future of ageing: developing a critical gerontology, *Sociological Research Online* 8(4) available at www.socresonline.org.uk/8/4/phillipson.html

Phillipson, C. (2004) Review article: Urbanisation and ageing: towards a new environmental gerontology, *Ageing & Society* 24: 963–972.

Robson, C. (1993) *Real World Research: A Resource for Social Scientists and Practitioner-Researchers,* Oxford: Blackwell.

Salari, S., Brown, B. and Eaton, J. (2006) Conflicts, friendship cliques and territorial displays in senior center environments, *Journal of Aging Studies* 20: 237–252.

Salari, S. and Rich, M. (2001) Social and environmental infantilization of aged persons: observations from two adult day care centres, *International Journal of Ageing and Human Development* 52(2): 115–134.

Sànchez-Jankowski, M. (2002) Representation, responsibility and reliability in participant-observation, in May, T. (ed.) *Qualitative Research in Action*, London: Sage, pp. 144–160.

Sheridan, D. (2002) Using the mass-observation archive, in Jamieson, A. and Victor, C. (eds) *Researching Ageing and Later Life: The Practice of Social Gerontology*, Buckingham: Open University Press, pp. 66–79.

Shore, B., Lerman, D., Smith, R., Iwata, B. and DeLeon, I. (1995) Direct assessment of quality of care in a geriatric nursing homes, *Journal of Applied Behaviour Analysis* 28(4): 435–448.

Stafford, P. (ed.) (2003) *Gray Areas: Ethnographic Encounters with Nursing Home Culture*, Santa Fe, NM: School of American Research Press and, Oxford, James Currey.

Wadensten, B. (2005) The content of morning time conversations between nursing home staff and residents, *Journal of Clinical Nursing* 14(s2): 84–89.

Wahl, H. and Wahl, G. (2002) Environmental gerontology at the beginning of the new millennium: reflections on its historical, empirical, and theoretical developments, *The Gerontologist* 43: 616–627.

Wallace, S. (2005) Observing method: recognizing the significance of belief, discipline, position and documentation in observational studies, in Holloway, I. (ed.) *Qualitative Research in Health*, Maidenhead: Open University Press, pp. 71–85.

Webb, E., Campbell, D., Schwartz, R. and Sechrest, L. (1966) *Unobtrusive Measures: Non-Reactive Research in the Social Sciences*, Chicago, IL: Rand McNally.

2

MORE THAN MEETS THE EYE

Using video to record the communication of older people with dementia in care settings

AILSA COOK AND GILL HUBBARD

OVERVIEW

This chapter presents findings and reflections from a body of research that has used video in the context of an inclusive, ethnographic approach to understand the communication of older people with dementia in care settings. It starts by outlining our rationale for using video and then goes on to review previous research using video to understand and disseminate social life. The methods used for gathering, analysing and disseminating video data are described in detail and practical, ethical and epistemological issues arising during the process discussed. The chapter concludes with a discussion of the added value that video can bring to research and with some recommendations for researchers considering adopting this approach.

OBSERVING OLDER PEOPLE

Over the past thirty years there has been a large body of observation research that has sought to document and understand the experiences and communication of older people, including those with dementia, in care settings. Researchers using systematic observation methods have recorded the nature and frequency with which residents engage in a wide range of pre-determined behaviours (e.g. Bowie and Mountain 1993; Ward *et al.* 1992) whilst researchers using participant observation methods have focused on understanding the meanings older people make of their lives in care settings (e.g. Golander and Raz 1996; Gubrium 1975).

A review of this research reveals that it is limited in what it can add to an understanding of the communication of older people with dementia. The cognitive impairments experienced by many people with dementia make communication difficult, especially using words (see Bourgeois 1991 for a review), leaving people with dementia more dependent on non-verbal channels of communication (e.g. Killick and Allan 2001).

Whilst previous research using systematic observation has generated a body of evidence about the kinds of non-verbal behaviours people with dementia use, it has tended to document behaviours within a very limited context, making interpretation of the meanings of those behaviours difficult. Furthermore, whilst researchers using participant observation have written about particularly notable non-verbal communicative behaviours and sought to make meaning of them (e.g. Golander and Raz 1996; Hubbard *et al.* 2003a; McColgan 2004) researchers using this approach have not generated detailed understandings of non-verbal communication. The limitations of both of these approaches for understanding non-verbal communication lead the authors to explore the possibility of using video to record the communication of older people with dementia.

VIDEO AS A RESEARCH TOOL

Video was identified as an ideal tool for advancing understanding of the communication of older people with dementia as it enables a permanent record of both verbal and non-verbal aspects of an interaction to be recorded in context. The researcher is able to review the recording time and time again, allowing for the intricacies of non-verbal and verbal communication to be observed, documented and interpreted in context. Review of research using video revealed that it is a relatively under used tool in social science research, rarely used by those seeking to 'make observations' of social life (Harrison 2002; Pink 2001; Prosser 1998). Video has been used to research non-verbal communication of infants (e.g. Gunning *et al.* 2004) and children (e.g. Doherty-Sneddon 2003). In the field of dementia, video has been used to record the wandering behaviour of people with dementia (Dewing 2004); to record group therapy sessions (Cheston 2002); to evaluate staff interpretations of people with dementia's non verbal behaviours (Athlin *et al.* 1990); and to evaluate the effectiveness of caring interventions (Kihlgren *et al.* 1996; Norberg *et al.* 1986; Phillips and Van Ort 1993).

Researchers who have used video have highlighted its potential as a research tool to record and analyse aspects of social life, and indeed to reflect on research process (Lomax and Casey 1998; Pink 2001; Rosenstein 2002). Researchers who have reflected on the methodological implications of using video have highlighted the extent to which the presence of the video camera distorts the phenomenon being observed (e.g. Heacock *et al.* 1996; Latvala *et al.* 2000; Lomax and Casey 1998;

Roberts *et al.* 1996; Rosenstein 2002). Roberts *et al.* (1996) recommend placing the camera next to a large object and recording over a prolonged period of time to minimise distortion. Similarly researchers have recommended collecting video data along side other data so 'realities' can be compared (Latvala *et al.* 2000; Morse and Pooler 2002).

Researchers working within an ethnographic approach have, however, found the influence of the camera less problematic, seeing it as just another feature of the research encounter to be reflected upon. Pink (2001) highlighted how the video camera shapes the researcher's identity and influences the way they communicate with the research participants, pointing out that this influence will change in different situations and in different relationships. Furthermore, Lomax and Casey (1998) demonstrate the possibilities for using the video recorded data itself to reflect on the influence of the camera in the construction of the research data. In their study of midwife encounters, Lomax and Casey (1998) analysed the ways in which the new mothers responded to the camera, and found that this reflected the ways in which they differentiated between what they considered to be midwifery business from social aspects of the visit.

A second key methodological issue identified in the literature on the use of video is the challenge of disseminating video data without compromising the anonymity of the research participants. Researchers who have used video data in research dissemination have tended to address this problem by negotiating the consent of the participants to use the film Pink (2001). However this approach is inherently problematic when working with a population whose capacity to give consent, and possibly more importantly to remember that consent, may be impaired.

Although researchers working with people with dementia over an extended time period have confidently obtained their consent to disseminate photos (Hulko 2005) and video recordings (Rose 2000), researchers working with individuals unable to give this kind of consent have been forced to find ways to disseminate research without visually identifying the participants. Thus, researchers have used technology to blur the faces of research participants (Dewing 2004); presented transcriptions of video recorded data (Cook 2003) and presented only the audio recording from video recorded data (Cheston 2002).

All of these means of dissemination, however, are limited in their ability to convey non-verbal aspects of interaction, prompting the authors to develop the approach to dissemination described in this chapter, which is to use actors to represent video recorded data (see also Hubbard *et al.* 2003b).

It is unsurprising, given the small body of research that has used video, that there is little guidance for researchers about to embark on video projects. In this chapter we seek to address this gap in the literature by outlining in detail the approach we have developed over the course of four research studies to gather, analyse and disseminate video data and present key findings and recommendations from this research.

DEVELOPING THE APPROACH

The approach to using video to gather, analyse and disseminate research on the communication of older people with dementia was developed over the course of four studies carried out by either one or both of the authors between 2000 and 2003. For most of this time we were both working at the University of Stirling, Ailsa on an ESRC funded PhD looking at the communication of older people with dementia in residential care, and Gill on an ESRC funded study into the quality of life of frail older people in care homes. Both projects involved observing the interactions of older people with dementia in care settings, and so early in 2000 we decided to work together to carry out a pilot study of the feasibility of observing and interpreting non-verbal communication of older people with dementia at a day centre using participant observation and a video camera.

The pilot study, which has been written up elsewhere (Cook 2001 and Hubbard *et al.* 2002), confirmed that video was both a useful tool for gathering data and acceptable to older research participants, including those with dementia. It highlighted the power and potential sensitivity of the recordings and the challenge of negotiating consent with older people with dementia, leading the authors to develop a protocol for obtaining process consent from the participants.

The approaches to gathering and interpreting data developed during this pilot were then rolled out with little change in our respective projects. Gill went on to observe the interactions of frail older people in twelve nursing homes and Ailsa carried out a video ethnographic study of the communication of older people with dementia in one residential care home. Over the course of these studies, we continued to meet regularly to talk about our respective projects and their emerging findings. During these discussions we both became frustrated with the inadequacy of the written word to convey non-verbal communication and so sought funding together for a fourth dissemination project. In this project we worked with actors to represent research findings on a key theme emerging in both our research projects, sexual expression, and produced a CD-Rom incorporating filmed excerpts of data with sociological text, to disseminate research findings visually.

In the following sections the approach developed to gather, analyse and disseminate video data is outlined in detail and key findings relating to the use of video from the four research projects discussed.

GATHERING VIDEO DATA BEFORE RECORDING

As highlighted in the introduction, the video camera was used in the context of an ethnographic, inclusive methodology to record verbal and non-verbal aspects of the interactions of older people with dementia in care settings. An important first stage of the research was to obtain consent from the participants to take part in the research and to be video recorded. Experience from the pilot highlighted the need to negotiate consent both formally with the participants at the start of the project and also to renegotiate consent on an ongoing basis every time the participants were recorded. The video camera and notebook were brought to the initial formal consent meeting to illustrate what taking part in the research would involve, at which point participants without dementia were asked to sign a consent form. Verbal consent was obtained for those participants with dementia who it was felt would not be able to remember that they had been recorded for the duration of the study (three years) and written assent was obtained from a family carer instead. At this point consent was also sought to show the recordings to actors so that they could dramatise the research findings.

Having negotiated consent formally with the participants the researchers carried out a number of sessions of participant observation without the video camera. This process was important for three reasons. Firstly, it allowed the researchers to get to know the participants and the routines and rituals ongoing in the setting. Secondly, it sensitised the researchers to the kinds of interactions and situations that it would be most interesting, as well as feasible, to video record. Finally, the time spent getting to know the participants and finding a shared language with which to talk about the research greatly helped in the negotiation of ongoing consent to record with the video camera.

Recording interactions

Once the researchers were familiar with the setting and the participants within it, they started using the video camera to record interactions in the setting. The camera was a small digital camera that could be positioned on a tripod or held in the hand. The first interactions recorded in the setting were mostly focused around the camera and the process of being recorded, as many of the participants were interested in the camera and excited by the prospect of being on film. During these interactions, after consent had been obtained from all those present, the participants were encouraged to handle the camera, to record each other and to watch these recordings back through the viewfinder. Unfortunately, many of the participants were unable to watch the recordings as they could not focus on the picture through the viewfinder and the use of a camera with an external screen would have greatly facilitated this process.

Having introduced the camera to the participants, the researchers started recording naturally occurring interactions in the setting. Interactions were recorded between residents whilst they were sitting together passing time or engaged in organised activities, such as playing board games, bowls or knitting. The way the researchers used the camera varied according to the physical environment in which the recordings were being made, the nature of the interaction recorded and the extent to which the researcher wanted to engage and be engaged with during the interaction. The best quality video recordings were made in environments with lots of light, little background noise and with the light behind the camera. The researchers recorded interactions whilst they were sitting, standing, or used a tripod depending on the number of people to be recorded and their positions relative to each other. The most straightforward interactions to record were between two people sitting next to each other as they could both be recorded in the same frame. In general, the more people present in an interaction, the more challenging it was to get a complete record of the interaction on camera, and in these instances the researcher would move the camera to record participants or groups of participants in turn, depending on who was the focus of the interaction at anyone time. This inevitably meant that parts of the interaction were not captured on camera and to compensate the researchers either recorded in pairs, with one recording and the other observing, or if working alone would look up from the camera so they could observe the interaction whilst recording.

A key finding to emerge from this process was that the engagement of the research participants with both the researcher and the camera was shaped by the approach taken to recording. When the researcher held the camera and looked through the viewfinder the participants tended not to include the researcher in the interaction, but were very mindful of the camera and frequently referred to the fact they were being recorded. When they spoke to the researcher it was to ask if they were still being recorded, or to joke that they were going to be on the television, as opposed to engaging with the researcher as a person. However, when the researcher maintained eye contact with the participants whilst recording they tended to focus on the researcher instead of the camera and include her in the interaction. When the recording was made with the camera on a tripod the participants often forgot they were being recorded all together and were only reminded when the researcher got up to check the recording or move the camera. Thus the presence of someone actively videoing the participants reinforced to the participants that they were being recorded. The researchers used these different responses to the camera to both remind the participants they were being recorded and to manipulate their own engagement in any interaction.

Using the video camera in these ways not only enabled the researchers to obtain good quality data on the verbal and non-verbal communication in the setting, but also was a process that many of the participants found enjoyable and meaningful. The ubiquity of video in society meant that the participants readily made meaning of the experience of being recorded in a way that they did not always of being observed when their actions were recorded using pen and paper. Thus participants (both male and female) would comment on the appearance of their hair and clothes on camera and joked that we should send the recordings to Hollywood. Some participants found the experience of being recorded very validating and would ask to be recorded whilst engaged in activities of particular significance to them, such as sitting with a partner or playing the piano. Many participants performed for the camera and one participant in particular used the presence of the camera to show her influence in the setting, acting as a director, calling staff and other service users in and out of the frame of the recording. Participants also played to the camera, often using physical humour such as exaggerated facial expressions and gestures. In these ways the participants used the camera to present a particular 'self'.

ANALYSIS OF VIDEO DATA

The active role that both the participants and researchers played in shaping the recordings had implications for the ways in which this video data could be analysed. As Lomax and Casy (1998) and Pink (2001) found, it was not possible to treat the data as a neutral representation of communication in the care settings. Instead the recordings were viewed as rich sets of data to be interpreted in the context of the broader understandings of the lives of the participants and the settings in which they were recorded. A key finding of the pilot study was that two researchers familiar with the participants could agree on the meaning of communicative behaviours (both verbal and non-verbal) observed in a care setting for older people with dementia and what is more, that staff shared those interpretations. The researchers were, however, keen to obtain the interpretations of the older participants themselves on the communication recorded and did this by playing back some of the recordings to the participants.

Reviewing the video recordings with participants

To elicit the interpretations of the participants themselves, the researchers played excerpts of video recorded data to participants (both staff and service users) several days after the recordings had been made. Only participants who had been part of the initial interaction were invited to review the recordings, which were shown in a quiet space in the care setting. As the participants watched the recordings the researchers asked them to comment on what they thought particular behaviours had meant. They were also asked to talk about how well the video recordings captured life in the setting.

As has already been reported (Cook 2001; Cook 2003) reviewing the recordings with the participants was a process that had to be managed very carefully. Many of the interactions recorded on video were rife with conflict and confusion. Participants were recorded getting confused, forgetting the names of people and objects as well as arguing with each other and gossiping about other service users. Given the sensitivity of the recordings a decision was made early on that only those participants present in the interaction should be able to watch them, however, this was something that was in practice very difficult to enforce. Staff and service users curious to see what was going on would regularly interrupt the review sessions making it necessary for the researcher to sit with their finger permanently poised over the pause button.

The challenges inherent in managing the review process made it more difficult to probe the participants for interpretations during the review. Whilst they readily commented on each other's hair and clothes, the participants with dementia were less able to comment on the behaviours observed on screen. This difficulty was confounded by the fact that several of the participants forgot that they had been recorded in the first place and one women was unable to recognise herself on screen. Participants without dementia, however, did make some interesting interpretations of the behaviours recorded on the video and on several occasions staff later offered further background information to explain why they thought participants had been acting in certain ways. For example, one woman had been recorded on video bullying other service users and making snide remarks about them to camera. Staff interpreted these behaviours as being expressions of insecurity prompted by changes in her living circumstances.

Whilst all participants said that they thought the video recordings captured what it was like to be in the setting, participants without dementia, both staff and service users, commented on how apparent both confusion and conflicts were on the video that they had not noticed when in the midst of the interaction. This was something that the participants with dementia did not explicitly comment on and whilst they enjoyed the activity it was difficult to encourage them to really engage with the content of the interactions, which given the extent of conflict in some interactions was possibly for the best.

Transcription and analysis

Transcription of the video recordings was a very time consuming process. The researchers watched the video and transcribed both the verbal and non-verbal communication of the participants, as well as making notes about the overall setting in which the interactions were occurring. The transcriptions of each recorded interaction were then cut and pasted into the ethnographic field notes from the relevant observation session to create a complete and detailed record for each fieldwork visit. These records were analysed qualitatively with the aid of the NVivo software package.

Review of the recordings over time highlighted the extent to which the process of transcribing the data was in and of itself a process of interpretation and analysis. There is an infinite amount of information present in even a few seconds of video recorded interaction and so the transcription of these interactions requires that the researcher constantly evaluate which bits of information are and are not relevant to the research. Decisions that both researchers made during transcription were shaped by the ideas they had about the data at the time, and so, just as the video recordings were shaped by the meanings the participants made of being recorded, the transcription of that data was shaped by the meanings the researchers were making of the lives of the participants and the setting. The permanent nature of the video record, however, meant that it was possible to go back to the data some months later and re-examine those interpretations in light of themes emerging in the analysis. Furthermore, the permanent nature of the video meant that it was possible to show the recordings to other members of the research team who had not been present during the observations. It was interesting to note that researchers not familiar with the participants or the setting tended to reach very different interpretations of the communication recorded, highlighting the extent to which interpretations were shaped by knowledge of the context in which they occurred. Thus transcription and analysis of the data were not static one-off events, but processes that unfolded iteratively over time and were intimately shaped by the researchers' experiences in the setting.

DISSEMINATING VIDEO DATA

Findings from these research projects have been disseminated in printed media (e.g. Cook 2003; Hubbard *et al.* 2002; 2003), however, as highlighted earlier in the chapter it was important to both researchers to find a way to disseminate the findings visually. The sensitivity of the recordings and the limited capacity of many of the participants to give consent meant that the video recordings themselves could not be disseminated as they compromised the anonymity of the research participants. Therefore the researchers worked with a film director, film crew and actors to represent the research findings dramatically so that the findings might be disseminated visually to a diverse audience in the form of an interactive CD-Rom.

The five-stage process taken to develop the CD-Rom, is described in detail in Hubbard *et al.* (2003b), and summarised in Table 2.1.

The most interesting stage in this process was stage three, when the researchers worked with the actors, film director and crew to dramatise and film the interactions.

Table 2.1 Developing visual dissemination materials

Stage	Activity
1	The researchers wrote up findings in the form of an academic paper on a key theme emerging from two observation research projects, sexual expression.
2	The film director transformed excerpts from the findings section of the paper into a series of scripts, one for each interaction. Where interactions had been video recorded, he also viewed these recordings.
3	Older actors were filmed acting out the scripts on location in a nursing home in Scotland with direction from the researchers.
4	The film director, editor and researchers worked together to edit the Footage into 16 short 10-50 second video clips.
5	Multi-media designers incorporated the video clips and academic text into an interactive CD-Rom.

The filming was done on location in an unused wing of a nursing home in central Scotland over the course of three days. Professional and student actors were employed by colleagues collaborating with us on the project from the Royal Scottish Academy of Music and Drama and the film director recruited students from the Film and Media course at University of Stirling to be the film crew. The researchers were present throughout the filming to offer guidance to both the director and actors to ensure that the dramatisations were as close to the interaction on which they were based as possible as well as appearing authentic. There were occasions, however, when it was necessary to change an aspect of the original observed interaction to ensure that the meaning intended by the participant would be apparent to the audience. For example, in one interaction a female participant referred to a fellow resident as a paedophile and it was felt that the meaning would be clearer if the term pervert was used instead.

A key challenge of the dramatisation process was to make the actors appear sufficiently old and frail to be credible. Although the actors were themselves older, the female actors in particular had spent the later years of their careers working hard to maintain a youthful image, dying their hair and going to the gym. Whilst they had brought in clothes that they believed to be old fashioned, it was only when they dressed in clothes borrowed from the laundry of the nursing home that they really took on the appearance of individuals who were reliant on others to maintain many aspects of their appearance. Some of the actors also struggled initially to relate to the characters they were playing and to understand their lives. This was overcome, however, by the researchers spending time with actors giving them some background about each character they were playing, as well as the events leading up to the specific interaction being represented.

The process of dramatising the research findings and developing the CD-Rom raises a key issue not only for the dissemination of research visually, but also for the dissemination of research on social life generally. The starting point for the CD-Rom was the paper that the researchers had written in a standard academic format. The limitations of this format for conveying the interactions that the researchers had observed became apparent as soon as the film director sought to transform the detailed excerpts of field notes presented in the findings section of the paper into a script. Even though the researchers had recorded verbal and non-verbal action in detail the process of recreating these interactions highlighted the partiality of the account and how important small details, such as where participants were sitting and what they were wearing, were to conveying the intended meaning. Furthermore, the process of working with the actors to help them understand the meanings behind the interactions they were recreating highlighted how ambiguous many of the meanings were and, again, how much the interpretations of the researchers were shaped by their intimate knowledge of the setting.

WHAT DOES VIDEO ADD?

The key benefit gained from the use of video in the projects described in this chapter was that using the video camera enabled the researchers to capture and analyse in detail aspects of non-verbal, as well as verbal communication that they missed whilst engaged as a participant observer in the setting. Whilst both researchers were able to take in a lot of detailed information about the non-verbal communication of the participants whilst observing in care settings without a camera, the video recordings captured the subtle intricacies of interaction, vital to interpret fully the sometimes confused interactions of the older participants with dementia. For example, the video camera captured the ways in which the participants moved furniture to encourage and discourage others from joining them and highlighted the use of non-verbal behaviours by many residents to communicate meanings that they could not verbalise. Analysis of the video recordings also enabled the researchers to examine changes in communication during an interaction and the influence of factors such as noise and pain on the ability of participants to engage with those around them. Furthermore, the permanent nature of the video recordings provided the researchers a valuable opportunity to revisit the raw data in light of themes emerging from the analysis.

The extent to which the participants engaged with and made meaning of the process of being recorded was an unexpected benefit of using the video camera in this research. Not only did the engagement of the participants with the camera facilitate the negotiation of informed consent, but the responses of the participants to the process of being recorded, which were themselves captured on film, provided unique windows into the selves of the participants.

CONCLUSION

Video is a powerful tool for researching social life that enables researchers interested in communication and interaction to gather and analyse detailed information about both verbal and non-verbal aspects of interaction. The power of the video recordings do, however, mean that it is a tool that needs to be handled with sensitivity on the part of the researcher in particular to ensure that the anonymity of the participants is preserved. It is also important for researchers about to embark on video research to be aware of the extent to which the recordings are shaped by the actions and interests of both the researcher and the participants. Thus video recordings do not constitute a 'true' record of the phenomenon under investigation, but are social and technological constructions and must be analysed accordingly.

REFERENCES

Athlin, E., Norberg, A., Asplund, K. and Jansson, L. (1990) Feeding problems in severely demented patients seen from task and relationship aspects, *Scandinavian Journal* of *Caring Sciences* 3(3): 113–121.

Bourgeois, M. (1991) Communication treatment for adults with dementia, *Journal* of *Speech and Hearing Research* 34: 831–844.

Bowie, P. and Mountain, G. (1993) Using direct observation to record the behaviour of long-stay patients with dementia, *International Journal of Geriatric Psychiatry* 8(10): 857–864.

Cheston, R. (2002) Re-presentation of people with dementia's words: top dogs and underdogs, paper presented at 'Dementia: An Inclusive Future' Symposium, the University of Stirling, 5 November.

Cook, A. (2001) Using video to include the experiences of people with dementia in research, in Wilkinson, H. (ed.) *The Perspectives of People with Dementia: Methods and Motivations,* London: Jessica Kingsley Publishers.

Cook, A. (2003) Using video to include the experiences of older people with dementia in research, *Research Policy and Planning* 21(2): 23–32.

Dewing, J. (2004): An investigation of wandering in older people with dementia living in a nursing home: ethics and research methods, paper presented to the 33rd Annual Conference of the British Society of Gerontology, University of Surrey, 9–11 September.

Doherty-Sneddon, G. (2003) *Children's Unspoken Language,* London: Jessica Kingsley Publishers.

Golander, H. and Raz, A. (1996) The mask of dementia: images of demented residents in a nursing ward, *Ageing & Society* 16: 269–285.

Gubrium, J. (1975) *Living and Dying in Murray Manor,* New York: St Martin's Press.

Gunning, M., Conroy, S., Valoriani, V., Figueiredo, B., Kammerer, MH., Muzik, M., Glatigny Dallay, E., Murray, L., TCS-PND Group (2004) Measurement of mother-infant interactions and the home environment in a European setting: preliminary results from a cross-cultural study, *British Journal of Psychiatry* 46: 38–44.

Harrison, B. (2002) Seeing health and illness worlds – using visual methodologies in a sociology of health and illness: a methodological review, *Sociology of Health and Illness* 24(6): 856–872.

Heacock, P., Souder, E. and Chastain, J. (1996) Subjects, data and videotapes, *Nursing Research* 45(6): 335–338.

Hubbard, G., Cook, A., Tester, S. and Downs, M. (2002) Beyond words: older people with dementia using and interpreting non-verbal behaviour, *Journal of Aging Studies* 16: 155–167.

Hubbard, G., Tester, S. and Downs, M. (2003a) Meaningful social interactions between older people in institutional care settings, *Ageing & Society* 23: 99–114.

Hubbard, G., Cook, A., Tester, S. and Downs, M. (2003b) *Sexual Expression in Institutional Care Settings: a Multimedia Research Document*. CD-Rom published by Department of Applied Social Science, University of Stirling.

Hulko, W. (2005) From doctor to 'silly patient': seeing beyond the disease label, *International Journal of Epidemiology* 34(1): 36–39.

Kihlgren, M., Hallgren, A., Norberg, A. and Karlsson, I. (1996) Disclosure of basic strengths and weaknesses in demented patients during morning care, *International Journal of Ageing and Human Development* 43(3): 219–233.

Killick, J. and Allan, K. (2001) *Communication and the Care of People with Dementia*, Buckingham: Open University Press.

Latvala, E., Vuokila-Oikkonen, P. and Janhonen, S. (2000) Videotaped recording as a method of participant observation in psychiatric nursing research, *Journal of Advanced Nursing* 31(5): 1252–1257.

Lomax, H. and Casey, N. (1998) Recording social life: reflexivity and video methodology, *Sociological Research Online* 3(2), available at http://www.socresonline.orq.uklsocresonline/3/2/1.htm

McColgan, G. (2004) Images, constructs, theory and method: including the narratives of dementia, in Innes, A., Archibald, C. and Murphy, C. (eds) *Dementia: An Inclusive Future? Marginalised Groups and Marginalised Areas of Dementia Research, Care and Practice*, London: Jessica Kingsley Publishers.

Morse, J. and Pooler, C. (2002) Analysis of videotaped data: methodological considerations, *International Journal of Qualitative Methods* 1(4) Article 3. Retrieved from http://www.ualberta.ca/-ijqm

Norberg, A., Melin, E. and Asplund, K. (1986) Reactions to music, touch and object presentation in the final stage of dementia: an exploratory study, *International Journal of Nursing Studies* 23(4): 315–323.

Phillips, L. and Van Ort, S. (1993) Measurement of mealtime interaction among persons with dementing disorders, *Journal of Nursing Measurement* 1(1): 41–55.

Pink, S. (2001) *Doing Visual Ethnography*, London: Sage.

Prosser, J. (ed) (1998) *Image-based Research*, London: Falmer Press.

Roberts, B., Srour, M. and Winkelman, C. (1996) Videotaping: an important research strategy, *Nursing Research* 45(6): 334–338.

Rose, S. (2000) Video diaries with people with dementia, workshop presented at the Journal of Dementia Care Conference, Edinburgh 4–5 April.

Rosenstein, B. (2002) Video use in social science research and program evaluation, *International Journal* of *Qualitative Methods* 1(3) Article 2. Retrieved from http://www.ualberta.ca/-jjqm

Ward, T., Murphy, E., Procter, A. and Weinman, J. (1992) An observational study of two long-stay psychogeriatric wards, *International Journal of Geriatric Psychiatry* 7: 211–217.

3

COMPOSING AND PERFORMING ETHNOGRAPHY
Doing observational research in the early 1980s

JULIA JOHNSON

INTRODUCTION

In this chapter I look back at some observational work I carried out twenty-five years ago in two residential care homes for older people (Johnson 1982; 1993). My purpose here is not to re-interpret the data but to re-examine the method I used. In particular, I want to focus on how I conducted the observational work (doing ethnography) in 1980/81, how I wrote it up (composing ethnography) in 1982 and, finally, how I presented it at the seminar (performing ethnography) in 2004. I want to look not just at 'what happens when we turn our observations into field notes and our field notes into stories' (Ellis and Bochner 1996: 19) but also what happens when we turn our stories into a performance. As we watched the video (or dramatic production) of Ailsa Cook and Gill Hubbard's ethnography during the seminar (see previous chapter), it occurred to me that an hour earlier I also had been performing my ethnography when I presented my paper.

BACKGROUND TO THE RESEARCH

The research compared two purpose-built residential care homes for older people, built in the early 1970s and run by the same local authority. The two homes were physically identical, being built to the same design, even down to the curtains, cups and saucers. How they differed was in terms of regime: one had converted the sluice rooms to small kitchens and was organised along small group living lines; the other was using the building as originally conceived for traditional living 'en bloc'. The purpose of the research was to investigate the relationship between the institutional environment and the lives of residents.

During the 1970s and early 1980s, participant and non-participant observational methods were a popular means of investigation in residential care homes for older people. Unlike today, the majority of homes were owned and run by local authorities and researchers had relatively easy access to them. In addition, because a great deal of daily life in many residential care homes was spent in 'public' spaces (Willcocks *et al.* 1987) which are open to surveillance, the words and deeds of both staff and residents were easily observable. Procedures regarding consent, which are commonplace today, were not so stringent. It is something of an irony that while much research of this kind was concerned with such matters as the extent to which residents' privacy was respected, being an observer felt like an invasion of privacy. Present day researchers may well express amazement that in 1981 I was granted access to bedrooms and bathrooms as well as communal living and dining areas.

DOING ETHNOGRAPHY

The positivist tradition, which was prevalent at the time, greatly valued systematic observation and its potential for revealing the truth. In order to conduct a systematic comparison between the two homes therefore, I chose, in addition to some interviewing, to use structured observation schedules which were originally designed and used by Gerald Evans *et al.* (1981) in their study of the management of mental and physical impairment in residential care homes. I used three observation schedules: two for observing staff and one for observing residents. Here I will focus on just two of these which I used to produce the data extract that is the subject of this paper.

The staff activity schedule

The staff activity schedule (see Figure 3.1) contained 14 columns. On this schedule it was possible to record what a member of staff was doing and to code it, with whom they were interacting and the nature of that interaction, the location of the activity, and the numbers of other staff and residents present. Each observation session was one or two hours long. At the beginning of a session, three members of staff were selected to represent each of the staff categories (supervisory, care, domestic). If more than one member of staff in a category was on duty at the same time, then a different member of staff was selected after 30 minutes so that a complete range of staff activity was recorded. Observation sessions took place on different days until the whole day from 6.40 am to 10 pm in both homes had been covered. In total therefore fifteen hours and twenty minutes of staff activity were observed in this way in each home.

The procedure for observing was as follows. The supervisory member of staff was observed first for 30 seconds. Then a further 30 seconds were used to record the observation, following which, one minute was allowed to locate the next member of staff when the procedure was repeated. Thus each member of staff was observed for 30 seconds every six minutes so that over a one-hour observation period, there would be 10 recordings for each. In total, 460 observations of staff activity were conducted in each home.

The resident activity schedule

The resident activity schedule (see Figure 3.2) also contained 14 columns so that what the observed resident was doing could be described and coded, any interactions with other residents or staff could be noted and coded, and the location of the activity and the number of people present could be recorded. Residents were observed during the following times: mid-morning; mid-afternoon; evening; and two mealtimes. All the residents in both homes were observed. They were divided into groups according to which lounge they used and those who did not use a lounge at all were included in a group whose lounge was nearest to their bedroom. At the start of each observation period the names of a group of residents were entered at random on the schedule. Each was then observed in turn following the same procedure as for the staff. At mealtimes, however, observations took place every minute rather than two minutes. Observations continued until each resident had been observed 7 times. In total 574 observations of resident activity were made in one home (19 hours) and 495 in the other (16.5 hours). On average each resident was observed 16 times in the first and 13 times in the second.

These schedules produced a substantial amount of qualitative and quantitative data. By way of example, in terms of quantitative data, it was possible to compare types of activity and types of interaction between staff and residents in the two homes and to find out whether residents were more or less likely to be interacting with one or two members of staff at a time. It was possible to draw comparisons about how the building was used: where activities such as eating took place, how often residents withdrew to the privacy of their bedrooms during the day and so on. These data could be triangulated with the qualitative data derived from the observation schedules.

Figure 3.1

STAFF ACTIVITY SCHEDULE:

Names ... Mot T / The / May
of
Staff ...

HOME ....

Date ... 9/9/81
Time 10:56 am to 11:08
Observer ... (S) (C) (D)

Initials of staff (1)	STAFF Code (2)	Activity(s) [description] (3)	Activity Code (4)	S - R Interactions [description] (5)	Name of Resident(s) involved (6)	Nature of R speech (7)	Nature of S speech (8)	S - S Interactions [description] (9)	Code of staff involved (10)	Nature of S - S Interactions (11)	Location (12)	No. Staff (13)	No. Residents (14)
The	C	Taking coffee to residents bedroom	FC		Mot T, Mrs H	NV NV	T T				B	1	1
May	A	cleaning residents bedroom	D		(..)						B	1	0
MoT	S	getting some medicine out of cupboard	A		(..)		TT				0	1	0
The	C	Taking coffee back to kitchen	FC		Nellie H, Henry S	I	TT				ML	1	22
May	A	cleaning resid bedroom	A		(Miss H)	T	T				B	1	0
MoT	S	attending to a resid in bed	FC		Mrs B H	T	T	Mrs Faz.	S	S	B	1	2
The	C	wheeling resid to toilet	FC		Ellen H, Polly	T	T				C	1	2

37

Figure 3.2

RESIDENT ACTIVITY OBSERVATION SCHEDULE:

Date ... Oct. 27th 1981 (Tuesday) ....

.... HOME

Time ... 10:12 am .... to ....

Observer ....

Resident Observed (initials) 1	Description of Activities 2	Activity Code 3	Description of Interaction 4	Nature of Observed R. speech 5	Nature of respondent R(s) speech 9	Name(s) of respondent R(s) 7	Description of Interaction 8	Nature of Observed speech 6	Nature of Ostaff speech 10	Staff Code 11	Location 12	No. Residents 13	No. Staff 14
PG	Sitting in chair dozing	DIS	X								L'	14	O
GP	Sitting in chair sleeping	DIS	X								L'	+	O
AG	Sitting in chair staring	DIS	X								L'	+	O
EH	In toilet	?	X				EH came back in. GP: "Shut the bloody door". EH: "Well I've not teeng hurt it. Then miles of cottages between & double please"				T	1	O
::	In chair dozing	DIS	X								L'	8	O
EG	In chair asleep	DIS	X				doorman (George tried to shut it) EH-prompted, light him on a chair + because he can't walk				L'	+	O
SM	Walking to toilet	M	X	H	SMH	SM	George still trying to shut door PG: "We'll fall if he moves" EH: At through handled in here"				C	1	O
R?	Watching Day Care arrive	R	X								L'	+	O
GP	Sitting tapping the door with stick	DL	"Can't he ruddy dance! Are you going out"				EG says leave it open. She can close it a little. There's a bit of a draft. (trying to compromise but someone has George Gr complain				L'	8	O
AG	Sitting staring	DIS					That'll do Eddy. (Closed so draft off and let stay on George.				L'	+	O

38

COMPOSING ETHNOGRAPHY

The resident observation schedule reproduced in Figure 3.2 was completed while I was observing a group of eight residents who shared a lounge in one of the homes in the study. I was in the lounge for one and half hours, sitting in a chair in the corner. When observing, there was no communication between me and those being observed. The observation session ran from 9.52 am to 11.28 am and the schedule in Figure 3.2 is one of 5 schedules completed during this period. It covers 20 minutes from 10.12 am to 10.32 am.

A literal reading of what is recorded on the schedule tells us that at 10.12, PG is sitting in a chair in the lounge, dozing and disengaged. She is one of seven residents. There are no staff there. There is no interaction. At 10.14, GP is likewise sitting in a chair, sleeping. No change. Two minutes later, AG is observed sitting in a chair staring. At 10.18, the observer searches out EH. She is in the toilet, alone. She returns to the lounge and at 10.20 there are now eight residents and no staff there. GP says 'Shut the bloody door.' EH says 'Well, I've got to come thro it.' This is a very hostile exchange. EH asks if everyone is warm and then decides to leave. EH knows GP can't move and purposely leaves the door open so that GP is in a draught. At 10.22, EG is asleep in the chair and GP tries to shut the door. Two minutes later, George [GP] is still trying to shut the door, whilst SM walks down the corridor to the toilet. PG comments 'He'll fall if he moves', and EH adds 'Although he walked in here.' At 10.26, PG is watching day care arrive. This is recreation. Two minutes later, George [GP] is sitting hoping that as she returns SM will close the door. This is the only occasion when the person observed is engaged in interaction. He says to SM: 'Shut the ruddy door. Are you going out?' this is a hostile interaction. EG says 'Leave it open.' This is because she herself is going to go out. EH says she can close it a little because there's a bit of a draught. She is trying to achieve a compromise between annoying GP and having some comfort for herself. At 10.30, AG is observed still staring, disengaged. EG says 'That'll do, Ed(d)ie [EH].' This is because the draught is off her but still on George [GP].

Looking back over this sheet, it is obvious that the structured nature of the schedule has placed considerable limits on the descriptive data. Whilst all the words and deeds have been recorded, there is no description of the participants themselves. By 1980, the more florid (and some might say very impressionistic) descriptions of people that one might find in ethnographic writing two decades or so earlier (for example, Townsend 1962) had passed. Nevertheless, there is quite a bit of information about the nature of the interaction between the residents, much of it hostile. Furthermore, when this sheet is put together with the other four schedules a story starts to emerge. Here is the account I wrote from the five completed schedules:

Parkview, Lounge 1: 9.52 am – 11.28 am, October

Mrs Hall, Miss Hartley, Mr Proctor, Mrs Goodacre, Mrs Miller, Mrs Garside, Miss Green and Mrs Whitehead are all seated in the lounge. Mrs Green is the only 'confused' resident. The rest are 'lucid' but not very mobile.

Mrs Hall enters the lounge in her wheelchair, very slowly; the other seven residents are sitting dozing. Miss Hartley tells Mrs Hall to 'hurry up and shut the door'. Mrs Hall goes over to her chair but can't get on to it. 'I can't reach it' she mumbles. Everyone ignores her. 'I can't manage it' she says again. 'Well you'll have to stop where you are then' replies Miss Hartley.

For the next 15 minutes everyone sits in silence and then Miss Hartley gets up to go to the toilet. As she goes through the door, Mr Proctor, who is sitting by it, growls 'Shut the bloody door.' Miss Hartley enquires whether everybody is warm enough. No-one replies so she leaves the door open. Mr Proctor tries to lean forward to close the door but can't reach it. Mrs Goodacre observes him rather anxiously. Nobody says anything. When Miss Hartley returns, she leaves the door open and Mrs Goodacre comments that if Mr Proctor keeps leaning forward like that, he will fall. Miss Hartley says she doubts it 'he managed to walk in here alright.' Miss Miller then gets up to go to the toilet and Mr Proctor tells her to 'shut the ruddy door'. At this point Mrs Garside chips in and says she can leave it open because she is just coming out. Miss Hartley who has found herself in a draft, asks Mrs Garside to leave the door half open (so that Mr Proctor will be in a draft but she will not). Mrs Garside complies with this request. This time Mr Proctor manages to shut the door and Miss Hartley shouts at him 'Leave it, no, leave it…you shouldn't have done that George, you know you're not cold…don't stare at me like that.' Mrs Miller returns and leaves the door open as instructed by Miss Hartley. Mr Proctor tries to lean forward again and is groaning. Mrs Goodacre enquires if he is alright but he does not answer.

'Speak to yourself' comments Miss Hartley.

'Well he can't talk' says Mrs Goodacre.

'Huh' says Miss Hartley 'He managed to talk to Edie alright.'

Miss Hartley then <u>tells Mr Proctor very firmly</u> to sit down. As he falls back into his chair, it squeaks. Miss Hartley says 'Was he grunting or was he breaking wind?'

'He seems bad' says Mrs Goodacre.

'He's alright' replies Miss Hartley 'He just wants the door shut.'

Miss Green gets up and goes to the dining room for coffee. Mrs Miller follows her. The rest stay behind and doze off for about ten minutes. Then Miss Hartley asks Mrs Goodacre if she could push the door to a bit (she herself is in a draft again). Mrs Goodacre ignores her. When Mrs Miller returns, Miss Hartley asks her to close the door a bit. Miss Miller <u>refuses</u> and leaves it open.

A care assistant comes in and helps Mrs Hall into a chair (she has been sitting facing the wall for an hour). The care assistant puts the television on and, as she leaves, Miss Hartley asks if she would mind closing the door as she is in rather a draft (she implies that the care assistant has been the cause of this). The door is closed, the test card comes up on the television and <u>everyone ignores it</u>. Miss Hartley gets up and goes to the toilet. She leaves the door open.

(Johnson 1982: 110–112)

Looking back at this, I can see that, in keeping with the positivist paradigm prevalent at that time, I have tried to remain as 'scientific' as possible. So for example, rather than providing personal descriptions of the residents, I have introduced them by using categories derived from the Crichton Royal Behavioural Rating Scale relating to 'lucidity' and 'mobility'. Nevertheless, I have given them names so that they become active subjects rather than the passive objects of my observations. I can also see that, although I have based this account strictly on my recordings of the residents' words and deeds, I have used my own words to turn it into a readable story and to try to recreate the atmosphere. Some of these I have underlined. For example, in the second paragraph, I have used the word 'mumbles' rather than 'says' followed by 'Everyone ignores her'. I could have said 'Nobody hears her' or 'No-one replies' or 'Everyone remains silent'. Likewise, there are many possible alternatives for other underlined words and phrases. In composing this account, therefore, I have first interpreted what was happening and then, albeit at an extremely rudimentary level, exercised some creative writing skills to convey those interpretations. To quote Carolyn Ellis, my 'written reality is a second-order reality that reshapes the events it depicts' (1996: 26).

In effect and in retrospect, from an hour and half of observing, a mini drama has been distilled. The chief protagonist in this drama is Miss Hartley and the story revolves around the antipathy between her and Mr Proctor and her attempt to use the door as a weapon against him.

PERFORMING ETHNOGRAPHY

Reading my account of Parkview, Lounge 1 out loud at the seminar was, I think, the first time I had done this. Unconsciously at the time, here was my opportunity to convey what I had perceived to be the reality of the situation. As I started to read, the lounge and the people came back to life. My words prompted my recall of the detail: I had been there and I could see what I was recounting. I no longer had to rely entirely on my written words. Now I could add intonations and emotions. I could be Miss Hartley shouting at George. I could be Miss Goodacre trying hesitantly to defend him. I could be Mrs Hall making a vain plea for someone to help her out of her wheelchair.

The question also arises as to why I chose this particular observation session as the focus for my paper. Why, out of the thirty-five and a half hours I spent observing residents, did I select this? Perhaps I selected it precisely because it did have a dramatic quality with a main character and a plot. It had the potential to entertain and my performance did raise a few laughs. It confirmed in people's minds that nothing much has changed which had not been my intention. My intention had been to demonstrate how this particular observational method could produce rich ethnographic data alongside quantitative data.

CONCLUSION

There has been considerable discussion about the merits or otherwise of revisiting old data. In 1997, Martyn Hammersley pointed to the socially constructed nature of data and suggested that there is limited potential in revisiting other people's data because the original researcher's 'cultural *habitus*' is not readily accessible to other researchers (Hammersley 1997). He was discussing the archiving of qualitative data and it being made available to other researchers. But does this argument apply to revisiting one's own data? Natasha Mauthner, Odette Parry and Kathryn Backett-Milburn, on the basis of returning to their own data, argue that it does (Mauthner *et al.* 1998). Their argument is that all data are epistemologically confined because they are unique products of the researcher and the researched created at a particular time. Joanna Bornat, however, takes issue with this post-structuralist line of argument. In returning to an interview she conducted thirty years earlier, she concludes that her interview exists in a time trajectory and is not a finished product. As such, it is open to re-analysis by herself and others (Bornat 2003; 2005; 2006).

In re-examining one's research as I have done, there is of course a danger of making oneself appear naive and foolish. It was not my intention to undermine the value of the research I conducted twenty-five years ago. I believe that it was useful and revealing and that it has been a contribution towards the development of better practices in residential care homes. I also believe that, at the time, this was a valid and reliable method of data collection, which was particularly suitable for a comparative study. In going back to it and looking at it through a different theoretical lens, I have gained new insights into how I produced and presented my ethnographic data. So I would agree with Bornat that my research material exists in a time trajectory which leaves it open to further analysis.

REFERENCES

Bornat, J. (2003) A second take: revisiting interviews with a different purpose, *Oral History* 31(1): 47–53.

Bornat, J. (2005) *Remembering and reworking emotions: the reanalysis of emotion in an interview*, keynote address, 5th International Symposium on Cultural Gerontology, Open University, Milton Keynes, 19–21 May.

Bornat, J. (2006) Secondary analysis of one's own and another's data, Seminar 2, (Practising QL research) *Qualitative Longitudinal Research: Principles, Practice, Policy*, ESRC funded seminar series, University of Leeds, 20 January.

Ellis, C. and Bochner, A. (eds) (1996) *Composing Ethnography: Alternative Forms of Qualitative Writing*, Walnut Creek, CA: Alta Mira Press.

Evans, G., Hughes, B., Wilkin, D. and Jolley, D. (1981) *The Management of Mental and Physical Impairment in Non-Specialist Residential Homes for the Elderly*, Research Report No. 4, Departments of Psychiatry and Community Medicine, University of Manchester.

Hammersley, M. (1997) Qualitative data archiving: some reflections on its prospects and problems, *Sociology* 31(1): 131–142.

Johnson, J. (1982) *Two Residential Homes for the Elderly: A Comparative Study*, MA Thesis, University of Keele.

Johnson, J. (1993) Does group living work? in Johnson, J. and Slater, R. (eds) *Ageing and Later Life*, London: Sage, pp. 120–127.

Mauthner, N., Parry, O. and Backett-Milburn, K. (1998) The data are out there, or are they? Implications for archiving and revisiting qualitative data, *Sociology* 32(4): 733–745.

Townsend, P. (1962) *The Last Refuge*, London: Routledge and Kegan Paul.

Willcocks, D., Peace, S. and Kellaher, L. (1987) *Private Lives in Public Places: A Research-Based Critique of Residential Life in Local Authority Old People's Homes*, London: Tavistock.

4

THE THEORY AND PRACTICE OF OBSERVATIONAL RESEARCH IN THE OUTDOOR SETTING

KATHERINE SOUTHWELL

OVERVIEW

This chapter outlines the basic concepts of environment-behaviour theory, describing their practical application for making observations in outdoor places. The potential and limitations of the theory and practice is discussed from a landscape architectural perspective. A range of observational techniques and their different modes of application are outlined, highlighting the 'transactionalist' approach for its role in overcoming a combination of conceptual, ethical and practical problems. Some observations of older people spending time in a forest place are used to illustrate the link between theory and practice.

BACKGROUND TO THE STUDY

When psychologists first began to realise the integrative nature of the relationship between human behaviour and physical setting some thirty or forty years ago, a new area of study emerged. This area became known as 'ecological psychology' – now termed environmental psychology. Subsequently, a 'transactionalist' perspective took shape and became influential to environmental design research.

Transactionalism provides a conceptualisation of the human occupied environment as a two-way relationship in which there is a cause-and-effect transfer between individual and environment. In this conceptualisation, the 'environment' is conceived of in ecological terms, providing a way of explaining the mutual relationship humans have with their environment. From the perspective of landscape architecture and urban design related research, transactionalism helps conceptualise the human/environment relationship by defining 'place' as an holistic unit.

Defining place

In the transactionalist approach 'place' is something with physical form that both shapes and symbolises the interactions which take place in it, and within which individuals set different goals and purposes for spending time in, and/or passing through it. Place is thus definable by three interrelated categories: a) physical attributes; b) the activities people engage in (behaviour); and c) people's perceptions (Canter 1977). In this way transactionalism offers a way of studying different aspects of the whole, in an approach that conceptualises the human/environment inter-relationship in terms of a 'cause-and-effect' transfer. This provides a useful framework for conducting an environment-behaviour observation study.

Environment-behaviour study helps identify how a physical environment supports, or interferes with, behaviours taking place in it. It also examines the side effects that a setting has on relationships between individuals or groups (Zeisel 1984). The overall aim is to generate data about people's activities and the relationships needed to sustain them. Whilst both person–environment and person–person relations can be identified, it is the person–environment category of observations that have most direct relevance to landscape architectural thinking because it shifts emphasis from 'the individual' to 'what is happening' contextualised in the physical setting.

When observing and recording what is happening in a physical setting, the behaviour is always seen within an environmental context: there is a surrounding environment and therefore always an environment-behaviour relationship. As well as recording what is going on, the aim of an environment-behaviour study is to present the findings in such a way that others will understand behaviour in a way not normally thought about (Bechtel *et al.* 1987). For environmental design research purposes, 'environment' can mean inside spaces such as hospitals and airports, or outside areas such as parks, plazas and streets. The focus area of observation depends on whether the research relates to architecture, landscape architecture or urban design. The design perspective overall aims to identify linkages between patterns of behaviour and the spaces they occupy. The skill lies in observing and recording those things that have the potential to make important design differences.

For design purposes, a distinction can made between 'general' and 'diagnostic' observation (Herschberger 2002). Both approaches to observation provide ways of watching the world 'in order to understand'. However, *diagnostic* observation aims to elicit 'vital' information from general background information. This helps generate an understanding about the nature of a design problem. For this, skill and experience is required for interpreting recorded observational data in order to 'diagnose' a problem, but also to recognize the problem exists in the first instance. On the one hand observational skill is required, on the other hand, design know-how is needed for analysing what is going on. It is when the two combine that observation becomes most useful.

THE UTILITY OF OBSERVATION IN LANDSCAPE ARCHITECTURE

The application of observational research methods in landscape architecture and related design disciplines is subject to the limitations of an underlying 'gap problem'. This is a conceptual problem impacting on the transfer of research knowledge into everyday design practice. According to Hillier (1996), this problem relates to a fundamental difference between research and design approaches: whereas 'scientific' research is traditionally concerned with how buildings and environments *are,* the [architectural] design approach is focused on how buildings/environments *might* be. In the landscape design approach the practitioner is typically focused on the spatial arrangement of a setting such as a street or forest park, its elements such as entrances, paths, together with fixtures such as seats and signage. This focus on physical form contrasts with the environment-behaviour research approach which records and observes 'events'.

Making observations

Those who have investigated the practical utility of behavioural observation in the landscape design process conclude that behavioural understandings are generated from observations of how existing places function, and that such observations need to be linked to physical form (Cooper-Marcus and Francis 1998; Sancar 1996). These authors emphasise the potential of environment-behaviour observation for the evaluative paradigm it brings to design. The implication is that by observing places in everyday use we can assess the quality of a place *as experienced* by the user and so inform our future decision making when designing new places.

When recording environment behaviours we can examine whether a place supports or obstructs people in carrying out their desired activity such as entering a place, sitting, and so on. This establishes the goodness of fit between what the users' needs are, and what the designer has provided. This puts emphasis on the *usability* of a design by which

47

approach we are asking not only 'what is going on', but also 'does it [the design] work?' Environment-behaviour observation carried out within this framework provides a particular 'lens' on the world, identifying layers of information about the background and detail of the physical context that indicate *what* people are doing and *where*.

The use of direct observation alone is, arguably, less effective when examining 'why' something is going on. Certain information can only be elicited through the interview approach. This helps uncover values, feelings, beliefs and so on. But whilst interviewing and observing are at opposite ends of the spectrum in terms of the way information is obtained, the two together provide a good impression of what is really going on. In the interview approach the researcher is obtaining a person's interpretation of what happened, direct observations 'in the field' can record what people *actually* did.

Sometimes observational 'evidence' is at odds with what people say. People do not always give an accurate account of events and at the same time, what a researcher observes may not predict very well what the observed are thinking (Herschberger 2002). This is explainable by the transactionalist approach which states that our place experience is shaped as much by the physical environment, as it is by our own goals and motives (and what we actually perceive) in a place. Consequently, when asking the question 'why' something is happening, behavioural observation is neither more nor less effective than interviews: it all depends on what you are looking for.

In an observation study, what you look for depends on what you want to do with the data (Zeisel 1984). The way information is presented also has an impact on whether or not it is used and so the form and content of the information presented must be suited to the audience (Bechtel *et al*. 1987). The subject matter that is most relevant to landscape architects is that which incorporates background landscape/townscape features and the elements within it, such as the paths – the materials used underfoot, how wide and how steep a path is, and so on. These details not only give form and structure to the human experience, they also shape the observation study.

The advantage of focusing observation on the environment-behaviour interaction as opposed to 'the individual' helps maintain anonymity of user/visitor/residents. This has become important for ethical reasons in the advent of privacy and data protection laws. This presents a topical and problematic area of debate in observational research.

Ethics

The visual tradition of environment-behaviour study has led to extensive photographic, film and videotape collections of material (Bechtel *et al.* 1987). The use of photographic recording is considered especially effective for outdoor spaces such as streets and plazas, where for example crowd activity can be condensed into a short viewing period. Time-lapse photography means that categories of observation can be defined and observed at a level of detail that is not possible in live observation because 'in the field' there is simply too much to take in. The use of film or photographic images help freeze-frame moments for detailed study, and to capture overall patterns that highlight where behaviour fits (or does not fit) with what an environment provides, for example seats put where no one wants to sit.

It is increasingly important to ensure anonymity if using image collections. This is of relevance even in the case where informed consent is gained, since people may not understand the consequence of sharing their images with a wide audience – whether in print or in presentations (Rivlin 2002). The use of data is however only one aspect of the ethical problem: the other relates to the methods used.

There is much justification for keeping observation 'secret' when studying what is happening in an open space setting. This helps avoid disturbing the naturalness of events. Although covert observation technically violates the principles of informed consent, it is commonly accepted that behaviour in open public spaces can be observed secretly, as long as anonymity is preserved. Discretion is called for always, but there are times where this is difficult when making observations outdoors in the open countryside setting because there may be nowhere to 'hide'. Observing from a distance is a typical solution to the problem, but depending on the sophistication and availability of technology, such as powerful camera zoom lenses, there is inevitably a loss of detail. The observer wanting to gain a good impression of what is going on, misses a range of sights, sounds and physical factors that influence behaviour. These include what people are saying/exclaiming, what they are looking and pointing at, touching, and so on. These are all important contributory factors that help diagnose an environmental design problem from the 'insider' perspective of the user/visitor.

The conventional approach to gaining an 'insider' perspective of events is through 'participant observation'. The general principle is to gain insights into what is going on by emphasising depth of study over breadth of data (Denscombe 2003). There are many versions of participant observation, ranging from simply 'being there' and maintaining an invisible role, to the overt approach which makes the researcher's presence explicit to people. The latter approach can also involve asking questions about people's intentions and actions.

This helps structure a naturalistic enquiry: 'being there' keeps the designer/researcher's role secret, so ensuring that observations do not affect the naturalness of a setting. This is most desirable to designers because it does not involve specialist social survey skills. It is within this paradigm of thinking that the doing of environment-behaviour observation in landscape design is best understood.

RECORDING OBSERVATIONS

The focus of environment-behaviour observation is on 'molar', as opposed to 'micro' activity. This eliminates eye blinks, for example, but includes important details of the physical context such as holding a handrail. Background factors such as what people are looking at, for example a distant view, are also considered relevant. In this way the factors that either help or hinder people in carrying out an activity are identifiable through people's behavioural response actions, and for diagnostic observation, these behaviours exist in relation to a design problem, such as signage causing confusion and awkwardness in people's behaviour.

The need for visual representation of observations is an important consideration when recording behaviours for landscape design purposes. The most useful tool for making observations in this respect is one that helps both 'in the field' (when recording observations), and in dealing with the data afterwards. Behaviour mapping method provides such a tool.

Behaviour mapping is the traditional approach to recording environment-behaviour observations. Environment-behaviour 'maps' are generated by plotting observations on a plan of an area. These observations may either record stationary activities in a space such as sitting and standing, or they may plot movement through space. The method (i.e. the process of making observations) is distinguishable from the 'product' (the environment-behaviour map), and together they provide a means of direct observation.

Direct observation

Cooper-Marcus and Francis (1998) describe behaviour mapping as activity mapping. They suggest that activities are observed for at least four separate half-hour periods, ideally on different days at different times. They suggest keeping a complete record of all that is happening in the space by age, sex, ethnicity, type of activity, and location. The method also suggests choosing a route that will pass sequentially through each part of the site on each walk-through, stopping to record (e.g. dots on a plan at the exact location of where people are in the space) or using a system of notation (e.g. dots with arrows to distinguish between stationary people, people on the move, male, female, and so on).

A systematic survey records *all* activities within, for example, a city plaza. Alternatively observations may be carried out in a selective manner using 'selective observation'. This filters out one activity group from all others, for example sitting behaviours, or focuses on one user type, such as older people. Observations can be made either on-the-spot or on the move, for example when tracking people. Observations can also be made using *indirect* methods.

Indirect observation

Role play is a useful method in the study of open space use. This can be used to examine different aspects of place from the perspective of different user groups such as walking person, horse rider, cyclist, wheelchair user, car driver, and so on by acting out different scenarios of use in a place (e.g. 'finding somewhere to sit'). Another approach is to use behavioural 'traces' such as footprints, worn away paths in grass, dropped litter and graffiti, to examine human/environment relations. Interviews are also an indirect method of observation, and as suggested above, these, together with trace observations, can combine in a multi-method approach to gain an holistic view of what is going on.

A combination of direct and indirect approaches is ideal for a thorough analysis of a place. Together, the two approaches can provide the level of detail required for *diagnostic* observation.

Diagnostic observation

For diagnostic observation where the aim is to elicit 'vital' information from general background information to analyse a design problem, Constance Perin's 'behaviour circuit' approach (Perin 1970) is particularly effective. The general principle is to break down one activity as a sequence of smaller behaviours that, from start to finish, construct the whole experience as a task based analysis. For example when 'going shopping', the sequence begins when leaving home, locking the door, crossing the road, going up and down curbs, catching the bus/getting in car, and so on.

The series of small activities required to structure a whole behavioural sequence (or 'behaviour circuit') can be elicited either by direct observation or through role play.

The larger unit of the activity to which Perin suggested her approach applies, is Roger Barker's 'behaviour setting' theory. This theory provides a way of categorising and examining everyday life in 'bite sized' bits (Bechtel *et al.* 1987). The approach conceptualises the world as holistic, 'ecological' units of space whose boundaries may or may not be physical. Rather, the different patterns of human activity create their own boundaries. Thus, in the example of 'going shopping', even though the movement of the shopper is influenced by the physical structure of the environment, the whole sequence of smaller activities is bounded by no single physical structure, but a sequence of indoor and outdoor experiences structured by the human-environment interactions taking place. This presents a conceptual difficulty for space-defining in landscape architecture: normally the designer's unit of analysis has physical form whereas this other type of space has 'experiential' rather than physical boundaries.

The need for methods to help designers conceptualise and visually represent spaces *as experienced* was first recognised some thirty years ago. A number of pioneering 'designer-researchers' have, over subsequent years, explored practical ways of introducing behavioural, psychological and perceptual dimensions to landscape and urban design (notably Lynch 1976; Alexander 1977; and Gehl 1987). Such authors have been important to the theoretical development of environment-behaviour study in the landscape architecture-related disciplines for integrating the environmental psychology dimension within design. Significantly, Lynch (1976) recognized that designers require practical techniques that are quick and simple to use when performing 'under the pressure of decision'. For this he identified the use of selective observation as the most suitable approach.

Selective observation

Selective observation contrasts with the comprehensive, systematic approach. Where the latter characteristically records all behaviours, selective observation reduces the scope of a study. The selective approach is, by its very nature, narrow but because of this it is rapid and effective (Lynch 1976). Selective observation considers the physical setting as something which blocks or facilitates intended human activities, so focusing on the 'cause and effect' phenomena that are related to *specific* activity types.

Selective observation operates at both large and small scales. At large scale, general patterns of behaviour observed within a frame of reference such as 'urban district' or 'street', remains constant whilst individuals are continually changing such as street shopping activity. At large scale the pattern may be considered 'static' because, subject to temporal change over the day/week/month/season, the overall pattern is relatively stable. This is distinguishable from detailed observations of people in close-up where recurring patterns of behaviour are more difficult to discern because at this scale behaviours are 'dynamic'. However, whether at large or small scale, selective observation helps by definition to narrow the scope of an observation study.

The selective approach is in turn subject to the influence of selective *perception*. This means that there is always a possibility that personal interests are influencing the data collected (Denscombe 2003). This is an added complication because the observer has to aim for objectivity. At the same time his/her role as intermediary between 'the world out there', i.e. the way it is experienced by others, and the need to act as 'interpreter', must be recognised.

When making observations using design methods, the interpretation of data is aided through the use of visual analysis. This type of analysis uses sketches and diagrams for processing information, and is an added dimension to the whole process. This is illustrated using some observations originally made within a wider wayfinding study (see Plate 4.1). This demonstrates the use of selective observation in combination with the behaviour mapping approach where it is used to evaluate signage provision at a forest park. The illustrations are extracted from an original study on 'The Effectiveness of Wayfinding Systems with Forest

Users' (Findlay *et al.* 2003) which was conducted by OPENspace Research Centre, Edinburgh College of Art/Heriot-Watt University for the British Forestry Commission.

The original forest wayfinding study focused on the use of signage as a key element in wayfinding. The study produced a set of tools for analysing wayfinding problems and to help point to appropriate design solution types. The study methods included semi-structured interviews and questionnaires together with behaviour mapping, role-play and spatial analysis. The behaviour mapping method was an integral part of the toolkit.[1] Application of the method is described below to demonstrate its use when evaluating the performance of an outdoor setting for wayfinding *with older people in mind*. Observations are extracted from the wider wayfinding study and presented here in the form of a stand alone, small scale study. These observations of older people spending time in an outdoor forest place are used to illustrate the linkage between theory and practice.

DESIGN EVALUATION (WITH OLDER PEOPLE IN MIND)

Two aspects of methodology are emphasised: i) the role of diagnostic observation for evaluating the design performance of a place for older people's use; and ii) the integration of selective observation with behaviour mapping method.

Some background theory – wayfinding for older people

The design of a wayfinding system to meet with older people's needs is important. Navigation is key for maintaining mobility and independence, and yet many older people find increasing difficulties with it due to declines in their cognitive, perceptual and motor abilities (Kirasic, 2000). In its wider definition wayfinding is a process that relates to cognitive mapping ability and spatial problem solving. For older people who have to concentrate harder on physical aspects of mobility, environmental wayfinding design must consider the fact that this user group has less energy and resources to spare for finding their way around.

---

[1] As part of the research outcome, the method became incorporated into a wayfinding analysis toolkit for forest managers. This is expected to be published in the near future.

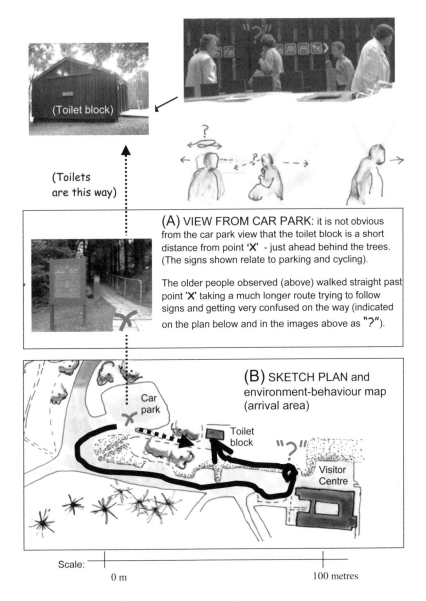

(Toilet block)

(Toilets are this way)

(A) VIEW FROM CAR PARK: it is not obvious from the car park view that the toilet block is a short distance from point 'X' - just ahead behind the trees. (The signs shown relate to parking and cycling).

The older people observed (above) walked straight past point 'X' taking a much longer route trying to follow signs and getting very confused on the way (indicated on the plan below and in the images above as "?").

(B) SKETCH PLAN and environment-behaviour map (arrival area)

Car park

Toilet block

"?"

Visitor Centre

Scale:

0 m   100 metres

Plate 4.1 Generating an environment-behaviour map using behaviour mapping method, selective observation and role play.

Putting theory into practice

Plate 4.1 illustrates how a wayfinding problem is identified through visitor behaviour and how an integrated selective/behaviour mapping method helps identify a design problem and a potential solution type using cause-and-effect diagnosis. A brief summary outline of the approach is described under the practices of 'survey', 'analysis', 'design':

Survey – (using selective observation)

A group of older people were observed in the arrival area of a forest park site. The group arrived by coach in the car park. They left their coach at the point marked with a 'X' on Plate 4.1 (see A and B) in the car park area. These visitors then took the route indicated by the solid black line arrow shown (see sketch plan B), moving towards the visitor centre. The group paused at the point marked "?". Here, the visitors appear discernibly confused, looking this way and that, pointing at the signs, looking and moving to the left and to the right, back and forth, displaying great uncertainty as to what to do next. These visitors were heard expressing their confusion aloud, saying 'where *are* the toilets?'. After much deliberation and hesitation, the visitors eventually found the toilet block either by trial and error (trying one direction, then the other) or by asking and/or following others.

Analysis – (using behaviour mapping, role play and spatial analysis)

The route from the car park to the toilets was subsequently analysed using role-play. The scenario 'finding toilets from car park' was used to act out this particular aspect of the visitor experience. This helped uncover not only the sequence of tasks required to complete the whole activity actually observed, but also the sequence of tasks that *could* have resulted in a different outcome. Notably, visitors could have followed a much shorter and simpler route from the car park *if* visitors had understood the site layout. This is indicated with a dotted arrow line from point 'X' to 'toilet block' (refer to Plate 4.1, B). The observed visitors, some of whom had obvious mobility difficulties, could have taken the shorter route, which is in fact a path specially designed for the mobility restricted, with a handrail and gentle slope. This route would have entailed walking a distance of approximately 20 metres

Figure 4.1 'How things might be'

distance rather than the longer, more convoluted 100 metres or so that these visitors actually took.

The observations provide 'evidence' that visitors were not aware of the shorter route option. In the physical setting there was neither a sign, nor a view of the toilet block from the car park because they were hidden from sight by the trees (see view, inset A on Plate 4.1).

Design – 'how things might be'

The observations highlight a design problem concerning site layout, sign placement and sign content. The type of analysis that the behaviour mapping method provides (integrating selective behavioural observation, role play, spatial analysis) suggests that the site layout is not being 'read' by visitors. The method does not analyse the role of sign content in the identified problem. However, in the wider wayfinding study from where these observations were extracted, behavioural evidence indicated that visitors generally found key facilities most easily where there was an obvious visual connection between what a sign said (e.g. 'toilets') and the 'object' sought (e.g. the toilet block). With this in mind, one can start to imagine some simple solution types such as clearing away tree growth so that visitors can actually see the toilet block from the arrival point. This helps envisage how the quality of the visitor experience on immediate arrival can be improved (see Figure 4.1).

The selective observation approach can be used in combination with behaviour mapping method to provide a fast method for identifying and analysing a design-related problem. By imagining 'how things might be' helps understand the potential of the current situation, and identifies 'cause and effect' relations between environment and behaviour. In this instance the confusion in visitor behaviour was attributable to the invisibility of the toilet block.

CONCLUSION

The potential and the limitations of the theory and practice of observational research in the outdoor setting has been the subject of discussion in this paper. A number of issues relating to the practicality of making observations in outdoor settings have been examined. Notably, the application of behavioural methods have been considered for their relevance to landscape architectural thinking, and the need to link behavioural observation with the physical arrangement of outdoor places.

The transactional perspective has been emphasised for its role as a background theory. Its usefulness was identified for providing an holistic framework for examining 'what is going on' as well as asking 'does it work?', and how things might be changed to improve the user experience. The transactional approach also provides a 'lens' for an observation study to help overcome some of the ethical implications of making observations. This is achieved by shifting focus from the 'individual' to the human-environment relationship. By this approach, anonymity can be retained, and the physical 'cause and effect' factors become the subject of discussion not an individual person, for example signage causing confusion and uncertainty.

Methods for identifying the cause-effect relations relevant to thinking about design are the techniques that are narrow in scope but provide depth of detail. When 'being there' in a place and observing what is going on in close-up detail, selective observation and behaviour mapping are two that have been highlighted for being effective for problem identification, cause-and-effect diagnosis, and for fitting with the designer's visual approach using photos and sketching.

The visual approach illustrated in the small scale study of older people in a forest place facilitates a way of seeing and thinking about open space and dealing with the data at the same time. A visual interpretation of observations helps analyse a design problem in detail in a diagnostic approach that demonstrates the utility of the theory and practice of observational research in landscape architecture and related disciplines. There remains however a conceptual difficulty in linking the spatial design of outdoor places with behaviour: an analytical framework which focuses neither on the person nor the physical environment but the interaction of the two, is inherently problematic. This strongly suggests the need for continuing debate and discussion about how to 'do' observation. In particular, theories and practices that help integrate spatial and behavioural ways of thinking within an overall visual approach require ongoing experimentation and dissemination.

REFERENCES

Alexander, C. (1977) A *Pattern Language: Towns, Buildings, Construction*, Oxford: Oxford University Press.

Bechtel, R., Marans, R. and Michelson, W. (eds) (1987) *Methods in Environmental and Behavioral Research*, New York: Van Nostrand Reinhold.

Canter, D. (1977) *The Psychology of Place*, London: The Architectural Press.

Cooper-Marcus, C. and Francis, C. (eds) (1998) *People Places,* 2nd edition, New York: John Wiley.

Denscombe, M. (2003) *The Good Research Guide For Small Scale Social Research Projects*, Maidenhead: Open University Press.

Findlay, C., Southwell, K., Ward-Thompson, C. and Aspinall, P. (2003) *The Effectiveness of Wayfinding Systems with Forest Users: Phase II – Identifying User and Site Information Needs*. A report for the Forestry Commission, to OPENspace – the Research Centre for Inclusive Access to Outdoor Environments, Edinburgh College of Art/Heriot-Watt University (unpublished report).

Gehl, J. (1987) *Life Between Buildings: Using Public Space*, New York: Van Nostrand Reinhold.

Herschberger, R. (2002) Behavioral-based architectural programming, in Bechtel, R. and Churchman, A. (eds) *Handbook of Environmental Psychology*, New York: John Wiley.

Hillier, B. (1996) *Space is the Machine: A Configurational Theory of Architecture*, Cambridge: Cambridge University Press.

Kirasic, K. (2000) Ageing and spatial behaviour in the elderly adult, in Kitchin, R. and Freundschuh, S. (eds) *Cognitive Mapping: Past,*

Present and Future, London: Routledge Frontiers of Cognitive Science 4, Chapter 10.

Lynch, K. (1976) *Managing the Sense of a Region,* Cambridge, MA: MIT Press.

Norman, D. (1988) *The Design of Everyday Things,* Cambridge, MA and London: MIT Press.

Perin, C. (1970) *With Man in Mind. An Interdisciplinary Prospectus for Environmental Design,* Cambridge, MA: MIT Press.

Rivlin, L. (2002) The ethical imperative, in Bechtel, R. and Churchman, A. (eds) *Handbook of Environmental Psychology,* New York: John Wiley.

Sancar, F. (1996) Behavioural knowledge integration in the design studio: an experimental evaluation of three strategies, *Design Studies* 17(2): 111–219.

Whyte, W. (1988) *City: Rediscovering the Center,* New York: Doubleday.

Whyte, W. (1980) *The Social Life of Small Urban Spaces,* Washington, DC: Conservation Foundation.

Zeisel, J. (1984) *Inquiry by Design. Tools for Environment-Behavior Research,* Cambridge: Cambridge University Press.

5

OBSERVATION IN THE CEMETERY

LEONIE KELLAHER

INTRODUCTION

Many might assume that cemeteries are the locus for the most inert data
conceivable and that observation would be the only method for fruitful
research at such sites. There is the common preconception that
cemeteries, intended as they are for the sequestered placement of the
dead, have been stilled and fixed in time and culture, that any interactive
enquiry – at least with the principal occupants of cemeteries – would be
futile in such places of mute immutability. Data on cultural shifts, on
motives underpinning memorialisation, on demographics, kinship
formations and structures, and around sentiments between the living
and the dead might well be considered out of reach, literally buried, in
the cemetery. At best, photographic records may be seen as the most
obvious material to collect, with other information being sought from
archival sources.

Until recently research in cemeteries has generally been conducted
within the disciplines of history and archaeology, with more or less
ancient memorial stones, grave markers and their inscriptions – to the
extent that words and motifs remain legible – being principal sources of
data. There is, however, a growing body of cemetery research to
illuminate such historical and archaeological observation that necessarily
limits dialogue with contemporary populations about the places, artifacts
and practices of commemoration. Through discourse with those who
attend graves we can move beyond such distanced observations with
approaches adopted in sociology and anthropology. However, the
boundaries between different strategies for data collection are often
permeable, and distinctions between 'purely' observational and
discursive approaches are fluid. This raises fundamental questions as to
the extent of the context setting required for the collection and
subsequent interpretation of data. For social scientists some
contextualisation is unavoidable since the laboratory is not, generally,
the milieu in which we work. As researchers adopting observational and
other qualitative – and quantitative – methods, we aim to undertake the
collection and analysis of material that generates findings termed

'credible' by Silverman (2001), and where validity, as discussed by Hammersley and Atkinson (1995) equates with confidence in the knowledge derived through interpreting data, whilst circumventing the 'certainty of truth' sometimes claimed for quantitative approaches.

My aim here is to consider how far observation on its own can generate data for description, analysis and, on occasions, for practice guidance and policy formulation, that are regarded as credible and valid. In what ways can contemporary accounts of rationales for choices that become manifest in the cemetery add to explanatory force and enhance levels of credibility? The term 'observation' in this instance is taken to mean visual surveillance of micro and macro cemetery landscapes and their populations, without the discursive and interactive input from the human sources social scientists take for granted when they conduct interviews and engage in ethnography.

Whilst I am focusing on a single study – of burial in London cemeteries at the end of the twentieth century,[1] I have to acknowledge the influence of material and findings from a related study concerning disposal of the dead through cremation.[2] This declaration, in itself, signals the difficulty – probably the impossibility – of isolating observation from contexts – social, cultural, temporal and spatial - especially where qualitative approaches are concerned. The cemetery study objective was to understand the place of the cemetery in twentieth-century UK society, with its range of cultural diversities. To set the scene for this discussion the aims stated at the start of the study are given here in detail. The first of these is the main focus through which to argue a case for observation with and without contemporary accounts from mourners.

- To analyse cemetery behaviour as an unexplored aspect of mourning and to examine how the experience of the cemetery landscape expresses the continuation of a social relationship between the living and the deceased as a process of identity construction as well as commemoration.

---

[1] ESRC funded project 1996; Cemetery as Garden: An ethnography of London Burial grounds and cross-cultural mourning practices with their policy implications. Ref: ESRC: 000236498.

[2] ESRC funded project; Environments of Memory: changing rituals of mourning and the personal, social and emotional implications. Ref: ESRC: 000239959.

- To trace how the symbolism encoded in landscapes and bereavement rituals link death, regeneration, the individual and society and reveal changes in the relationships between person and nature. To develop knowledge regarding the emergence of a new paradigm of nature as partner, active and alive, not passive and manipulable (as in mechanistic models of nature/culture), assessing its expression in new models of 'appropriate' burial landscapes which are more rugged and wild.
- To clarify existing knowledge on the evolution of individual and collective identities through understanding how the cemetery reflects continuities and changes in social values, demographic patterns and community relations of family, class, gender, age and ethnicity in English society which, in turn, provide the stimulus and context within which ritual mourning behaviour takes place.
- To recommend practical policy and practice applications regarding the use of historic and contemporary cemeteries, based on understandings of present and future needs by studying what they mean to people who plan them, maintain them, mourn in them, visit them, befriend them and study them.

As social anthropologists, the main research strategy entailed ethnography, which is to say, observation over time and encounters with those acting on and within the location. This was research into an area hitherto unexplored and whilst a great deal of preliminary and pilot work had preceded the bid and the start of fieldwork, it was by no means certain that people would co-operate in talking about their reasons for grave tending and the ideas they entertained about the grave, the deceased and any afterlife, as well as their family and domestic circumstances. So whilst we hoped to enter into dialogue with people in the cemetery, we speculated that if this did not transpire we could, at least, gather useful material though observational strategies. The expectation was, nonetheless, that, having gained the agreement of the cemeteries' management as to how we could proceed, some discussion would be possible and that cemetery professionals could add to accounts from mourners, as we termed visitors.

We anticipated the introduction of several quantitative exercises, for example to note the volume and character of attendance at different weekly, special ritual and seasonal times. The denominational and socio-cultural features of each cemetery research site also invited collection of comparative observations. However, discussion with those visiting and tending graves would be necessary if we were fully to meet the objectives. How else to understand something of the influences that led to particular forms and styles of monument, for the presence or absence of religiosity and other aspects of identity across a life-span? The following section outlines how we approached the research and the sources of data from which findings were ultimately drawn.

THE DATA COLLECTED

In designing the bid the character and 'catchment' of London cemeteries was carefully researched and a decision taken to select sites that would allow a range of socio-cultural and denominational customs to be studied. Six sites were selected for focused study though, as work progressed, a number of subsidiary sites were included. Agreement was reached with the managers of each cemetery to undertake the work, and as to the approaches that would be sensitive to those using the particular cemetery. Doubts as to whether visitors would be prepared to discuss the issues we had identified as relevant were expressed along with the insistence that approaches be delicate and low key. Tape recording was deemed too intrusive. Access to records was granted and cemetery staff members agreed to give their perspectives. These sources would provide some 'baseline' data to fall back on should mourners be reluctant to engage.

Acknowledging that respondents at each site represented a biased group, in that they were those who visited cemeteries rather than stayed away and were more likely to be included in our study if they were frequent visitors, we completed a full calendar year of observations with many more encounters than we had anticipated. Not all of these yielded data to address the more profound research questions, but a quarter gave extremely rich material (Francis *et al.* 2005). A few of these people gave information on several occasions and a small number were visited at home, where memorialisation also takes place. The 1500 contacts across all the sites over a calendar year were retrospectively grouped according to three intensities of communication combining observation and dialogue.

Level 1 (28% of 1500): Limited observation of people's activities at a grave with minimal conversation.

Level 2 (47% of 1500): Relatively brief interviews in which information was obtained about visitor-mourner practices at the grave; an aide memoir/check-list was completed.

Level 3 (25% of 1500): In-depth interviews in which information was gathered about feelings, reflections and dispositions as to the meaning of grave visiting and cemeteries; observation of activities at the grave, with conversation, discussion and questions/answers about the grave and the mourner's activities.

This means that well over 300 people (level 3) told us about their ideas and motivations, as well as about family history and traditions, religious and secular influences on long term and pragmatic decision making. The discussions were often intense, immediate and intimate with information and explanation being imparted and elicited in a concentrated manner, sometimes over just 20 minutes. It should be said that it was often relatively straightforward – though not without its emotional challenges – for mourner and researcher to engage, through the powerful presence of the grave, from which cues for discussion were taken. Although people agreed to talk for 'just a few minutes' they invariably continued for much longer. In this connection it should be said that the importance of locating this enquiry at the place where some, but by no means all, bereaved people choose to visit to remember people to whom they have been close in life, cannot be underestimated. As noted, the cues provided by the grave plot itself, and the mourner's activities in shaping, materially and cognitively, this micro landscape within the macro landscape of the cemetery, led the dialogues that came to constitute our most significant body of data, against the backdrop of data from the 1200 less intense contexts (levels 1 and 2).

The data collected also took account of silences, postures and dispositions during activities. It should not surprise us that mourners at a grave-site are in reflective mode and that intervals of silence were common, to be deemed significant. By their own admission, many visit the cemetery and the grave in a deliberate move to place themselves close to the memory – and the remains – of the deceased. Talking to the deceased was mentioned with great frequency, though with some embarrassment. These exchanges were sometimes described verbatim, more often paraphrased. People's ideas on such profound issues as an after life, about religion, their own motives and the like, were so readily and clearly formulated and fluently offered that we concluded they had been rehearsed vocally or silently many, many times as people struggled to come to terms with events. This is just one of the evaluations we came to attach to a habit that emerged consistently across each site and culture. It illustrates, however, the very permeable line separating observation and interaction between respondent and researcher. In the following section analyses and data that culminated in central findings are presented in order to suggest how far observations can stand alone as the base for credible and valid findings and, then, the differences data from contemporary narrative might make.

FINDINGS: LANDSCAPES AND SOCIAL RELATIONSHIPS

The first of the aims – *The experience of cemetery landscapes and mourners' expressions of continued social relationship between the living and the deceased* – is brought under focus by separating its two elements, landscapes and relationships, and considering each at the macro and micro levels that reflect, among other phenomenon, the interrelations posited at the outset, between the individual and wider society. Ethnographic approaches entailed a mix of observation and discourse, with some reference to documents, records maintained at cemetery sites and archives.

Cemetery landscapes

The distinction between macro and micro landscapes was proposed in the bid and subsequently proved central to several analytic strands. Each individual grave plot emerged as a micro landscape managed and organised by the mourner though, importantly, their options and choices were shaped by wider sets of influences such as law, rules, regulations, norms and fashions. In aggregate these micro landscapes formed the macro – the cemetery. These often extensive landscapes encompass past and contemporary mortuary practices and so reveal the connections over time between the living of a particular society or culture and its dead. Whilst separating 'landscape' and 'relationship' findings is problematic, some points can be made at this juncture.

The micro/macro analytic, as played out on the ground between grave owners and cemetery management, not infrequently in contested form, was pivotal to identity construction for mourners as they worked to re-establish their post-mortem lives. For professionals, cemetery managers, staff, funeral directors and clergy as they represented civic, administrative, commercial and religious aspects of society, the contest between individual and aggregate was also a matter of identity. The outcomes of tension varied from one cemetery to another depending on factors such as management style and resources, ritual and customary requirements, but the consequence was the overall character of each landscape. We put forward the finding for a cemetery code or syntax as the idiom in and by which mourners styled their plots. This could be, and often was, deciphered by professionals who then had to put aside their understandings to execute their duties towards the collective. But how far did observation alone take us down these analytic paths?

These open, ostensibly public places are not easily overlooked, so we might argue that everyone observes cemeteries from time to time and so understands enough of their purpose, if not of meanings. In the UK we are accustomed to seeing large expanses of land sited at the peripheral approaches to large conurbations – often close to the ring roads that surround cities and large towns. These are spaces that we 'understand' to be burial grounds, areas that have been turned over to the placement of the dead. Many of the largest and more obvious grounds, established in the nineteenth century and expanded in the post Second World War years are often described, not least in local media, as sterile wastelands of regimented, grey and toppling monuments, dangerously liable to vandalism and other disorders. As such they are likely to be contrasted – unfavourably – to churchyards that traditionally lie at the heart of rural communities; small, with monuments haphazardly set amongst mature trees and plantings of shrubs. These are the balanced and moderated settings where death may be approached, seen as co-existing with life of the vegetative variety and sheltering wild life endangered elsewhere. Places for burial and disposal of the dead take a number of other forms that are more or less visible, appearing in media of various kinds, local and national press and, increasingly, internet and websites. Even those who do not concern themselves with matters of mortality and afterlife are likely to register the presence of such sites.

These are the macro landscapes that we see in the UK, either prominently, or more 'invisibly'. Many would recognise them for what they are, burial grounds for the dead of settled groups. We would know this because, in Western Europe, such spaces and places have a similar 'legibility', which is to say, they would generally be made up of individual plots, customarily with a marker, even if only a simple mound. These plots would be positioned and made accessible in such a way that a more or less defined 'grid' would be in evidence. The analogy of neighbourhoods, streets and dwellings is frequently invoked when people observe these sites more closely. The several cemetery sections are usually chronologically ordered so that observation shows changing styles of memorialisation across the decades. The nineteenth-century cemeteries, with their front-row mausolea for the wealthy Victorian families, set along paved avenues of mature trees, sometimes with recent additions of municipally designed flower beds, can appear as parkland, country or suburban estate. Indeed, this was invariably the intent of the Victorian landscapers and public health campaigners who influenced the establishment, design and operation of cemeteries. Even where these ideals were overlaid or toppled by later twentieth century municipal bureaucracies, to the eye cemeteries can still convey aspects as ordered grounds or romantic wildernesses, for example Highgate Cemetery in North London. So far we can make the case that observation of the most cursory kind is likely to have contributed to degrees of awareness, interest and concern. At the same time, it is difficult to avoid the possibility that assumption, if not informed interpretation, has already intruded into 'observation'.

The micro landscapes of individual grave plots, typically combining a stone or durable memorial and a space for planting or placing flowers, are also legible at several levels. The form and elaboration of the grave, along with the inscriptions generally identify the deceased and their kinship contexts. Where this is not clear, meaning might be deduced in relation to social status; common graves for paupers or the indigent being understood, in British culture, as unidentified or taking a 'back row' position away from the main ceremonial routes. The converse is true of the larger and more impressive graves that reveal something of Victorian wealth and status. The more transient features such as the plantings and floral tributes at graves and other sites for disposal – for instance at columbaria containing ashes – can also be revealing. As with the images and languages inscribed on the stones, plantings may be associated with different cohorts, styles and cultures. Thus, the cemetery site can be 'read' at many levels. The details may become obscured over time, but a rudimentary 'code' is legible even when unsupported by discursive explanation.

A number of texts have derived their analyses of cemeteries from findings that did not entail contemporaneous dialogue with mourners. Most recently Ken Worpole (2003) describes and discusses the architecture of the Western cemetery from megalithic times to the present. Others include Curl (1993), Sloane (1991), and Strange (2005) to name only a few from many. Their findings and deliberations are widely regarded as significant and accepted as credible and valid. The frames within which their data are positioned are documentary and visual, reflecting the past rather than commenting on the present. The same might be said of the archaeological record. These disciplines triangulate using confirmatory or disconfirmatory data from a range of inert sources to establish validity. This is not to say that they cannot and do not anticipate future patterns or forms of cemetery arrangements, or that findings based on historical data are unchallengeable because these lie in the past. Nor is it to say that analysis of contemporary cemetery material does not also draw on findings of preceding decades and centuries or other places and cultures of mourning.

Exploration of contemporary western society is now frequently approached through more or less fine-grained ethnographic methodologies, albeit triangulated with quantitative or survey data. The processual detail so derived is seen as giving access to levels of explanation that extend beyond surface manifestations. Before giving an account of findings that can be considered as falling under the 'social relationships' heading, it is useful to note what Runciman, in his Treatise on Social Theory (1983) said about how we understand social phenomenon. He argues for three levels of understanding, employing, interestingly in this context, the example of the Albert Memorial in Kensington Gardens, London. The basic level he identifies is the visual, whereby one observes the edifice and describes it as having certain dimensions and being constructed of particular materials that give colour and allow the form to be shaped using special techniques. Runciman proposes that this much is possible through visual observation, without introducing other interrogatory strategies. He goes on to argue, however, for two other levels of understanding if we are to comprehend the significance of the structure in terms of its purpose and place in its time. I would add that any grasp of symbolic meaning will be enriched – though complicated – by experiential accounts. In the following section mourners' accounts are considered as they talked about their visit to the grave of someone who had been important to them – often as a co-resident spouse, parent, sibling or child – followed by the conclusions drawn from this data on social relationships.

Social relationships, the living and the dead

If it is the case, and many social scientists have so argued (for example, from Hertz (1907), to Bloch and Parry (1982)), that places and modes of post-mortem disposal reflect a society's ideas about the living and the dead, where may such a connection be located? Is it in the macro landscape, representing a duty of remembrance on the part of society as a whole to generations past? Or does responsibility lodge closer to home, in the immediate present and past and between those who have shared the personal relationships indicated and inscribed on stones or manifest through grave tending visits? What difference does a refocusing of the research 'lens' – from the socio-macro to the individual and personal – make to the credibility of any analysis and the validity of data on which it is based and how far does observation remain an adequate approach?

One set of findings closely connected to this aspect of the research aims concerns the debate between the stages theory of bereavement, in which people pass through a series of states and eventually reach the point of renewal when fresh investments in future connections with others can be formed (e.g. Parkes 1972), and the more recently argued continuing bonds proposition (Klass *et al.* 1996). The socio-micro and socio-macro data and analysis are presented to preface a summary of our finding in this area.

In response to the researcher's opening gambit: 'Would I be intruding if I were to ask you about your visit here, today?' people spoke in a matter-of-fact way about their routines, habits and then about rationales, moving on to their tentative beliefs and ideas. They frequently commented on their present, everyday lives and sometimes on the 'lives' the deceased now 'experienced'. They also reflected on life before bereavement and made comparison with their new circumstances. The devastating fracture death had wrought was usually recounted with resignation and sadness rather than distress. Many of these people, particularly those who were visiting the grave of a partner or co-resident kin, described visiting routines and habits developed for grave tending that included the deceased and allowed the living to reflect on and practice a new and evolving self alongside an earlier self as spouse, adult child or sibling. Elderly widowers cleaned and tidied the gravestones, tended the grave gardens and reported having assumed the household tasks their wives had performed all their married lives. A widower in his seventies gave this account:

> 'We were married forty years. Things at home are the same as always. But I'm not quite so efficient with the cleaning. I used to help. I got so good with the ironing and doing the shirts that I went to see the doctor – it's not the sort of thing a man does.'

Another said:

> *'I have more memories at home (than in the cemetery). We lived in our home for thirty-three years and for twenty-five years before that in another house. I did the gardening myself. Now I have lots of chores: the washing and cleaning and cooking my own meals. I do it just the same as she did, and my gardening too.'*

Bereaved partners at all the cemetery sites had often chosen to adhere closely to the jointly established weekly routine of domestic tasks. This acceptance of ongoing responsibility for care of the home seemed to underpin many of the largely secular rituals of remembrance. The regular and routine nature of housework and other home-related chores offered the opportunity to keep busy with distracting tasks as when this widower said: *'When I feel down, I get to work.'* Another seventy-five year old who had redecorated the house according to his dying wife's instructions acknowledged that: *'She worked it out so I was kept busy.'* The purposeful assumption or continuation of domestic routines permits a consolidation of the living self and the deceased other. It reveals continued personal growth in the achievement of a necessarily expanded self as the transition to a role of widower takes place.

Whereas older men who were accustomed to helping around the house may find comfort and security in caring for the home, the corresponding adjustment can be more challenging for widows. But for many a similar reinforcement of self appeared to be achieved through managing the home single-handedly and through extending this new necessity to the cemetery. A woman in her late seventies used the conversation to set out her domestic standards when she said:

> *'A wife (of my generation) is different from younger wives today. In my age group, to be a wife was to cook, clean, to be domestic. He went to work, decorated the house and gardened ... I hate to think (the memorial and grave-garden) is mucky, dirty, not tended to. If you are clean and tidy in your home, you keep the things which belong to you clean and tidy. It is like looking after him at home – like doing the washing, ironing and cooking. There is something here that belongs to him and I have to take care of it for him. If I didn't come I would feel that I was neglecting my duties as a wife.'*

These kinds of routine activities were often described as reciprocal since the surviving spouse was now maintaining the deceased's new 'home' – as well as preparing the places where they would one day resume co-residence as a couple. Even those older men and women who had 'moved on' in the sense that they had formed new relationships, sometimes marrying, retained the past, along with their earlier identities, as essential to their present. A widow in her seventies, now remarried to a widower explained:

> *'With a new relationship, you have to take on board the other person's life and their partner. You can't push it away because of jealousy. In a way you have to share him with her and to listen when he talks of her. That's the difference between being a divorcee and a widow – she was the best part of his life, she walks with him everyday, she was the mother of his children.'*

Such insights may be indicated, but will not be inscribed, on a gravestone. The significance of the home and domestic routine, along with the way in which the grave becomes a new 'home', can only be picked up through their reiteration of intimate and complex thoughts.

A different idiom was likely with older people from groups where religion featured more prominently. For the Cypriot, with an Orthodox Christian background, a large family network was likely to be mentioned as the point of connection with the deceased. This grandmother said: *'Home is where your loved ones are – dead or alive.'* And a middle-aged couple visiting the wife's parents' grave said:

> *'It's important we remember our dead, not just for religion but because we are a family. The family blood ties are very important. You cannot and never should forget your own blood. Just as they took care of us ... it's now our turn to keep their memory alive.'*

Whilst such sentiments of reciprocity and mutuality across generations were also strongly expressed by indigenous Londoners, they tended to be cast in a less collective, more individual mode. *'She was a good mother and she deserves this (the grave cleaning, decorating) from her daughter.'*

Before moving to a discussion of how this kind of narrative material may add to observation of social relations an expanded idea of the data that shaped findings about interrelationships between the living and the dead, is offered.

Parents who had lost children often expressed the need to remain connected, in its strongest form. For example the mother of twins, one of which had died as a baby said: *'I always knew it was something I did not want to forget or get over.'* Another couple described their decisions about their child: *'We chose an area where the children's graves are together. Here we do not have to speak. It is a shared experience. The other parents know our story and we know theirs... .'* Other parents spoke of continued interdependence with a child who had died as a stillborn infant, a baby or a young adult. They visited frequently and left presents on birthdays that, they explained, were suited to the age the child would now have reached. Other bereaved parents were said to give presents on such occasions and surviving or new siblings would be included on these commemorative occasions. In these ways, the dead were involved in ongoing family life.

Not all the interrelationships that were re-enacted through the grave were benign. An adult son said of his deceased father: *'He was not a man you could be close to. I do now talk to him about my problems, I do try and communicate ... maybe the flowers show it, they are all fresh, colourful flowers. All I know, if I come over here ... I feel a lot better when I go.'* This remark, along with those of others, suggests that a distant and difficult relationship at the end of a parent's life could, even in death, be improved and moved closer to an imagined ideal – in this case through cemetery attendance.

Through such examples of spoken insights we can access something of the micro-socio aspects of interrelationships between society's living and dead. As with micro landscapes of individual grave plots, the larger scale can be read from the individual. For instance, the variable appearance of each of these cemeteries, serving groups with a range of socio-cultural requirements and customs is explained with reference to levels of cultural and generational emphasis placed on the individual and/or family as the 'unit' for mourning and remembrance. Data on the collective 'unit' of remembrance was collected mainly through observation of visiting patterns. Again, there was variation across the cemeteries. The quantitative work – counting visitors on the days special to each of the ethnic groups – was revealing. On for example, Mothers' Day, Eid, Easter, Christmas, Yom Kippur, mixed, three-generational groups were observed in very great numbers at all sites. This was in contrast to the more subdued visiting groupings – of one or two individuals – apparent on 'ordinary' days and suggested different sets of motives and rationales. Whilst the public and perhaps didactic purposes might be construed from the observations, confirmation came from individuals in some of the large visiting parties. *'We come here to tell the children where they are from'* said a Bangladeshi father, clarifying the generational and migrational connotations the statement contained. A white, east end London grandfather gave a very similar account for the large group he led, saying that it was an occasion when the older members of the family could tell the younger ones how working life and community had been in the past.

We might observe the clustering of children's graves in municipal cemeteries and note that this is a recent development by observing the contrast with Victorian child burials that, insofar as they are recorded on memorials – were with family elders. The elaborate and costly design of a contemporary memorial stone for a child will further indicate the now unusual event of child death – in western culture at least. The Muslim graves will belie this for recently settled groups where infant mortality remains high. However, the sentiments expressed by parents who maintain and update their child's persona, can only be partially understood through the materiality of bonds.

OBSERVING, DISCUSSING AND EXPLAINING THE CEMETERY

To some – admittedly heuristic – extent, certain findings that may be said to fall under the headings 'landscapes' and social relationships' have been disentangled here. Observation has been emphasised ahead of the research strategy of collecting contemporary accounts and commentary on actions on the significance to mourners of the micro landscape of the grave and the larger scale setting of the cemetery. At this point, we ask: is observation enough and to what particular social science ends? When must we add to observation so that it moves towards explanation that can ground policy and practice? This raises questions, central to Runciman's argument for three levels of understanding (1983). It may be fair to say that, even without engaging in conversation with mourners who visited to attend to graves of family, and some who were looking for the graves of forebears they had not personally known, we could have exceeded Runciman's first level of understanding. This is true insofar as we could deduce much about the meanings cemeteries and individual grave plots hold for contemporary society as a whole and for individuals through visual observation on its own. Some points of understanding at this level are now cited, briefly and by no means exhaustively.

Through observing the several macro and micro terrains, the chronologies and forms that characterised the different cemetery sections and grave styles; and by examining archives, the legislation, burial records and by getting wider perspectives from professionals – our hesitant fall-back position at the start of the project – we could have made the following statements:

- Cemeteries occupy considerable, though peripheral, areas of land that is now (though was not at the nineteenth century time of establishment) valuable, implying that the dead occupy a place of some significance for society.
- Monuments, similarly, continue to represent a not insignificant investment – economically and emotionally – on the part of surviving family.
- Investments of materials and time represented by and within the cemetery suggest that a 'contract' of some kind exists between the living and the dead.
- Groups demonstrate solidarities – of community, ethnicity, faith, class/status and of generational concern on certain occasions.
- Nature and culture appear in differential balances over the decades; romantic wilderness becomes an acceptable replacement for ordered municipality once personal connections have lapsed. But historic sites are more than 'museums'.
- Recent burials appear to be the focus of more and different kinds of attention that earlier ones.
- Mourners are active for up to a decade following a burial, when attention appears to drop away.
- Infant and child deaths have a very different distribution and consequent significance now as compared to the mid- and late Victorian era.
- Mourning customs now reflect a more restrained, less expressive reaction to death, than was the case up to the First World War.

Thus, we could comment on the significance of cemeteries for society at least in the immediate term. We may also, however, point to the abandoned nature of some cemeteries, the overgrown dereliction, the sunken graves and broken monuments to suggest that society, if not the individual family, or some of its members, has broken its links with those generations that lie beyond personal acquaintance.

Such findings would speak more to the 'letting go' paradigm of bereavement (Parkes 1972), than to frames for 'continuing bonds' (Klass *et al.* 1996), a question with contemporary significance, with which we framed the data in order to make some of our recommendations for policy and practice. When, however, we start to take account of comments from the living as to their perspectives and experiences, this observational ground starts to shift. Professionals and mourners took rather different positions however. Commentary from professionals reinforced a 'letting go' not just in what they said but in how they expressed themselves. They were generally more in favour of the staged version of bereavement that culminates in letting go of the dead, recovery from loss and formation of new relationships. They voiced reservations about bereaved people who visited 'too' frequently, especially after years had elapsed since the significant death.

The weight of all the data, not least the unambiguous accounts offered by many partners and parents for whom grave tending had become a routine part of everyday life, about family, friends and others who preferred they 'forget', drew us to say that commitments to the dead and to the site of burial extended well beyond the first decade. They could be retrospective over several generations and for Friends Groups could entail financial commitments to memorialise preceding, symbolically connected communities. The low-key nature of habitual grave tending and the tentative explorations of 'lost' descendents, left few markers of their concerns. At the same time, it might be countered that our cemetery-based sample would be biased in the direction of continuing bonds since the very fact of visiting committed people to this rather than letting go. The two positions are not incompatible. Earlier frames of reference such as Hertz's Rites of Passage (1907) argue for a reincorporation of the bereaved back into the life of society as the culmination of mourning rituals, in other words, for a 'letting go'. But Van Gennep (1909) and others also suggest that mourning can also be a search for ways of allowing the dead to assume a legitimate place in society.

Our data supported a paradigm of bereavement that emphasised social interdependence across generational time and across the life–death divide. Had we restricted our analysis to the data observed, we may well have drawn the other conclusion – that mourning is bounded by a personal commitment that excludes wider society. Discussion with those most directly concerned served to illuminate, but also complicate. We concluded, though, that without the volume of verbatim comment from mourners we could not have presented findings that pointed to valid concerns about current policy questions. The re-use of graves within a limited time-span following the last burial is a case in point. At the very least, because we could produce expressions of concern and responsibility spanning three or four generations, our recommendation for a period of 75 to 100 years should elapse carried some weight.

This is just one example of the value of collecting accounts from the living. But it also has to be admitted that much was learned through recorded observation. Interestingly, however, it is only when the narratives of the living are cited that the debate takes on an urgency. The observational data provoked fewer challenges from interested parties, such as practitioners and professionals, than did interpretation of the contemporary accounts. It may be, however, that the excavation of the present – in terms of uncovering mourners' rationales for and understandings of visiting and the cemetery itself – in places specially set aside for 'disposal' of the dead, generates tension. Putting the dead away, in the sense that archaeology, for example, may assume, with its essentially distanced research approach is at odds with the close focus that talking to lay people in the cemetery itself, as they resist the sequestration of their dead that society appears to demand.

REFERENCES

Bloch, M. and Parry, J. (eds) (1982) *Death and the Regeneration of Life,* Cambridge: Cambridge University Press.

Curl, J. (1993) *A Celebration of Death,* London: Batsford.

Francis, D., Kellaher, L. and Neophytou, G. (2005) *The Secret Cemetery,* Oxford: Berg.

Hammersley M. and Atkinson, P. (1995) *Ethnography: Principles in Practice,* 2nd edition, London: Routledge.

Hertz, R. ([1907] 1960) *Death and the Right Hand,* New York: Free Press.

Klass, D., Silverman, P. and Nickman, S. (1996) *Continuing Bonds: New Understandings of Grief,* Washington, DC: Taylor & Francis.

Parkes, C. (1972) *Bereavement: Studies of Grief in Adult Life,* Harmondsworth: Penguin.

Runciman, W. (1983) *A Treatise on Social Theory, vol I, The Methodology of Social Theory*, Cambridge: Cambridge University Press.

Silverman, D. (2001) *Interpreting Qualitative Data: Methods for Interpreting Talk, Text and Interaction*, Thousand Oaks, CA: Sage.

Sloane, D. (1991) *The Last Great Necessity: Cemeteries in American History*, London: Johns Hopkins University Press.

Strange, J. (2005) *Death, Grief and Poverty in Britain, 1870–1914*, Cambridge: Cambridge University Press.

Van Gennep, A. ([1909] 1960) *The Rites of Passage*, Chicago, IL: University of Chicago Press.

Worpole, K. (2003) *Last Landscapes: The Architecture of the Cemetery in the West*, London: Reaktion Books.

THE AUTHORS

Andrew Clark is a Research Fellow in the Leeds Social Sciences Institute at the University of Leeds

Ailsa Cook is a Lecturer at the RBS Centre for the Older Person's Agenda at Queen Margaret University

Gill Hubbard is a Senior Research Fellow in the Cancer Care Research Centre at Stirling University

Julia Johnson is a Senior Lecturer in the Faculty of Health & Social Care at The Open University

Leonie Kellaher is Emeritus Professor and Director of the Centre for Environmental and Social Studies in Ageing at the London Metropolitan University

Katherine Southwell is an Honorary Research Fellow at the Edinburgh College of Art